CRIME

ITS CAUSE AND TREATMENT

CRIME

ITS CAUSE AND TREATMENT

by

CLARENCE DARROW

GYAN

Published by

GYAN

Gyan Publishing House
5, Ansari Road
Daryaganj, New Delhi-110002
Phone: 011-47034999, 9811692060
E-mail: books@gyanbooks.com

Distribution Network
gyanbooks.com
India, USA, Canada, UK, Australia, France

ISBN : 978-81-212-6101-2 (PB)
First Published, 1922

2nd Impression 2021

Printed at: Gyan Press, Delhi.

Crime
Author: Clarence Darrow

CRIME

ITS CAUSE AND TREATMENT

BY

CLARENCE DARROW

1922

PREFACE

This book comes from the reflections and experience of more than forty years spent in court. Aside from the practice of my profession, the topics I have treated are such as have always held my interest and inspired a taste for books that discuss the human machine with its manifestations and the causes of its varied activity. I have endeavored to present the latest scientific thought and investigation bearing upon the question of human conduct. I do not pretend to be an original investigator, nor an authority on biology, psychology or philosophy. I have simply been a student giving the subject such attention as I could during a fairly busy life. No doubt some of the scientific conclusions stated are still debatable and may finally be rejected. The scientific mind holds opinions tentatively and is always ready to re-examine, modify or discard as new evidence comes to light.

Naturally in a book of this sort there are many references to the human mind and its activities. In most books, whether scientific or not, the mind has generally been more closely associated with the brain than any other portion of the body. As a rule I have assumed that this view of mind and brain is correct. Often I have referred to it as a matter of course. I am aware that the latest investigations seem to establish the mind more as a function of the nervous system and the vital organs than of the brain. Whether the brain is like a telephone exchange and is only concerned with automatically receiving and sending out messages to the different parts of the body, or whether it registers impressions and compares them and is the seat of consciousness and thought, is not important in this discussion. Whatever mind may be, or through whatever part of the human system it may function, can make no difference in the conclusions I have reached.

The physical origin of such abnormalities of the mind as are called "criminal" is a comparatively new idea. The whole subject has long been dealt with from the standpoint of metaphysics. Man has slowly banished chance from the material world and left behavior alone outside the realm of cause and effect. It has not been long since insanity was treated as a moral defect. It is now universally accepted as a functional defect of the human structure in its relation to environment.

My main effort is to show that the laws that control human behavior are as fixed and certain as those that control the physical world. In fact, that the manifestations of the mind and the actions of men are a part of the physical world.

I am fully aware that this book will be regarded as a plea or an apology for the criminal. To hold him morally blameless could be nothing else. Still if man's actions are governed by natural law, the sooner it is recognized and understood, the sooner will sane treatment be adopted in dealing with crime. The sooner too will sensible and humane remedies be found for the treatment and cure of this most perplexing and painful manifestation of human behavior. I have tried conscientiously to understand the manifold actions of men and if I have to some degree succeeded, then to that extent I have explained and excused. I am convinced that if we were all-wise and all-understanding, we could not condemn.

I have not thought it best to encumber the book with references and foot-notes, for the reason that statistics and opinions on this subject are conflicting and imperfect, and the results after all must rest on a broad scientific understanding of life and the laws that control human action. Although the conclusions arrived at are in variance with popular opinions and long-settled practice, I am convinced that they are old truths and are in keeping with the best thought of the time.

I am aware that scientifically the words "crime" and "criminal" should not be used. These words are associated with the idea of uncaused and voluntary actions. The whole field is a part of human behavior and should not be separated from the other manifestations of life. I have retained the words because they have a popular significance which is easy to follow.

CLARENCE DARROW.

Chicago, August 1, 1922.

CONTENTS

CRIME
ITS CAUSE AND TREATMENT

I

WHAT IS CRIME ?

THERE can be no sane discussion of "crime" and "criminals" without an investigation of the meaning of the words. A large majority of men, even among the educated, speak of a "criminal" as if the word had a clearly defined meaning and as if men were divided by a plain and distinct line into the criminal and the virtuous. As a matter of fact, there is no such division, and from the nature of things, there never can be such a line.

Strictly speaking, a crime is an act forbidden by the law of the land, and one which is considered sufficiently serious to warrant providing penalties for its commission. It does not necessarily follow that this act is either good or bad; the punishment follows for the violation of the law and not necessarily for any moral transgression. No doubt most of the things forbidden by the penal code are such as are injurious to the organized society of the time and place, and are usually of such a character as for a long period of time, and in most countries, have been classed as criminal. But even then it does not always follow that the violator of the law is not a person of higher type than the majority who are directly and indirectly responsible for the law.

It is apparent that a thing is not necessarily bad because it is forbidden by the law. Legislators are forever repealing and abolishing criminal statutes, and organized society is constantly ignoring laws, until they fall into disuse and die. The laws against witchcraft, the long line of "blue laws," the laws affecting religious beliefs and many social customs, are well-known examples of legal and innocent acts which legislatures and courts have once made criminal. Not only are criminal statutes always dying by repeal or repeated violation, but every time a legislature meets, it changes penalties for existing crimes and makes criminal certain acts that were not forbidden before.

Judging from the kind of men sent to the State legislatures and to Congress, the fact that certain things are forbidden does not mean that these things are necessarily evil; but rather, that politicians believe there is a demand for such legislation from the class of society that is most powerful in political action. No one who examines the question can be satisfied that a thing is intrinsically wrong because it is forbidden by a legislative body.

Other more or less popular opinions of the way to determine right or wrong are found to be no more satisfactory. Many believe that the question of whether an act is right or wrong is to be settled by a religious doctrine; but the difficulties are still greater in this direction. First of all, this involves a thorough and judicial inquiry into the merits of many, if not all, forms of religion, an investigation which has never been made, and from the nature of things cannot be made. The fact is, that one's religious opinions are settled long before he begins to investigate and quite by other processes than reason. Then, too, all religious precepts rest on interpretation, and even the things that seem the plainest have ever been subject to manifold and sometimes conflicting construction. Few if any religious commands can be, or ever were, implicitly relied on without interpretation. The command, "Thou shalt not kill," seems plain, but does even this furnish an infallible rule of conduct?

Of course this commandment could not be meant to forbid killing animals. Yet there are many people who believe that it does, or at least should. No Christian state makes it apply to men convicted of crime, or against killing in war, and yet a considerable minority has always held that both forms of killing violate the commandment. Neither can it be held to apply to accidental killings, or killings in self-defense, or in defense of property or family. Laws, too, provide all grades of punishment for different kinds of killing, from very light penalties up to death. Manifestly, then, the commandment must be interpreted, "Thou shalt not kill when it is wrong to kill," and therefore it furnishes no guide to conduct. As well say: "Thou shalt do nothing that is wrong." Religious doctrines do not and clearly cannot be adopted as the criminal code of a state.

In this uncertainty as to the basis of good and bad conduct, many appeal to "conscience" as the infallible guide. What is conscience? It manifestly is not a distinct faculty of the mind, and if it were, would it be more reliable than the other faculties? It has been often said that some divine power implanted conscience in every human being. Apart from the question of whether human beings are different in kind from other organisms, which will be discussed later, if conscience has been placed in man by a divine power, why have not all peoples been furnished with the same guide? There is no doubt that all men of any mentality have what is called a conscience; that is, a feeling that certain things are right, and certain other things are wrong. This conscience does not affect all the actions of life, but probably the ones which to them are the most important. It varies, however, with the individual. What reason has the world to believe that conscience is a correct guide to right and wrong?

The origin of conscience is easily understood. One's conscience is formed as his habits are formed — by the time and place in which he lives; it grows with his teachings, his habits and beliefs. With most people it takes on the color of the community where they live. With some people the eating of pork would hurt their conscience; with others the eating of any meat; with some the eating of meat on Friday, and with others the playing of any game of chance for money, or the playing of any game on Sunday, or the drinking of intoxicating liquors. Conscience is purely a matter of environment, education and temperament, and is no more infallible than any habit or belief. Whether one should always follow his own conscience is another question, and cannot be confounded with the question as to whether conscience is an infallible guide to conduct.

Some seek to avoid the manifold difficulties of the problem by saying that a "criminal" is one who is "anti-social." But does this bring us nearer to the light? An anti-social person is one whose life is hostile to the organization or the society in which he lives; one who injures the peace, contentment, prosperity or well-being of his neighbors, or the political or social organization in which his life is cast.

In this sense many of the most venerated men of history have been criminals; their lives and teachings have been in greater or lesser conflict with the doctrines, habits and beliefs of the communities where they lived. From the nature of things the wise man and the idealist can never be contented with existing things, and their lives are a constant battle for change. If the anti-social individual should be punished, what of many of the profiteers and captains of industry who manipulate business and property for purely selfish ends? What of many of our great financiers who use every possible reform and conventional catch word as a means of affecting public opinion, so that they may control the resources of the earth and exploit their fellows for their own gain?

No two men have the same power of adaptation to the group, and it is quite plain that the ones who are the most servile and obedient to the opinions and life of the crowd are the greatest enemies to change and individuality. The fact is, none of the generally accepted theories of the basis of right and wrong has ever been the foundation of law or morals. The basis that the world has always followed, and perhaps always will accept, is not hard to find.

The criminal is the one who violates habits and customs of life, the " folk-ways " of the community where he lives. These customs and folk-ways must be so important in the opinion of the community as to make their violation a serious affair. Such violation is considered evil regardless of whether the motives are selfish or unselfish, good or bad. The folk-ways have a certain validity and a certain right to respect, but no one who believes in change can deny that they are a hindrance as well as a good. Men did not arrive at moral ideas by a scientific or a religious investigation of good and bad, of right and wrong, of social or anti-social life.

Man lived before he wrote laws, and before he philosophized. He began living simply and automatically; he adopted various "taboos" which to him were omens of bad luck, and certain charms, incantations and the like, which made him immune from ill-fortune.

All sorts of objects, acts and phenomena have been the subjects of taboo, and just as numerous and weird have been the charms and amulets and ceremonies that saved him from the dangers that everywhere beset his way. The life of the primitive human being was a journey down a narrow path; outside were infinite dangers from which magic alone could make him safe.

All animal life automatically groups itself more or less closely into herds. Buffaloes, horses and wolves run in packs. Some of these groups are knit closely together like ants and bees, while the units of others move much more widely apart. But whatever the group may be, its units must conform. If the wolf gets too far from the pack it suffers or dies; it matters not whether it be to the right or the left, behind or ahead, it must stay with the pack or be lost.

Men from the earliest time arranged themselves into groups; they traveled in a certain way; they established habits and customs and ways of life. These " folk-ways " were born long before human laws and were enforced more rigidly than the statutes of a later age. Slowly men embodied their " taboos," their incantations, their habits and customs into religions and statutes. A law was only a codification of a habit or custom that long ago was a part of the life of a people. The legislator never really makes the law; he simply writes in the books what has already become the rule of action by force of custom or opinion, or at least what he thinks has become a law.

One class of men has always been anxious to keep step with the crowd. The way is easier and the rewards more certain. Another class has been skeptical and resentful of the crowd. These men have refused to follow down the beaten path; they strayed into the wilderness seeking new and better ways. Sometimes others have followed and a shorter path was made. Often they have perished because they left the herd. In the sight of the organized unit and the society of the time and place, the man who kept the path did right. The man who tried to make a new path and left the herd did wrong. In its last analysis, the criminal is the one who leaves the pack. He may lag behind or go in front, he may travel to the right or to the left, he may be better or worse, but his fate is the same.

The beaten path, however formed or however unscientific, has some right to exist. On the whole it has tended to preserve life, and it is the way of least resistance for the human race. On the other hand it is not the best, and the way has ever been made easier by those who have violated precepts and defied some of the concepts of the time. Both ways are right and both ways are wrong. The conflict between the two ways is as old as the human race.

Paths and customs and institutions are forever changing. So are ideas of right and wrong, and so, too, are statutes. The law, no doubt, makes it harder for customs and habits to be changed, for it adds to the inertia of the existing thing.

Is there, then, nothing in the basis of right and wrong that answers to the common conception of these words? There are some customs that have been forbidden longer and which, it seems, must necessarily be longer prohibited; but the origin of all is the same. A changing world has shown how the most shocking crimes punished by the severest penalties have been taken from the calendar and no longer even bear the suspicion of wrong. Religious differences, witchcraft and sorcery have probably brought more severe punishments than any other acts; yet a change of habit and custom and belief has long since abolished all such crimes. So, too, crimes come and go with new ideals, new movements and conditions. The largest portion of our criminal code deals with the rights of property; yet nearly all of this is of comparatively modern growth. A new emotion may take possession of man which will result in the repeal of many if not all of these statutes, and place some other consideration above property, which seems to be the controlling emotion of today.

Crime, strictly speaking, is only such conduct or acts as are forbidden by the law and for which penalties are prescribed. The classification of the act does not necessarily have relation to moral conduct. This cannot be fixed by any exact standard. There is no straight clear line between the good and bad, the right and wrong. The general ways of determining good and bad conduct are of little value. The line between the two is always uncertain and shifting. And, in the last analysis, good or bad conduct rests upon the "folk-ways," the habits, beliefs and customs of a community. While this is the real basis of judging conduct, it is always changing, and from the nature of things, if it could be made stable, it would mean that society was stratified and all hope of improvement dead.

II

PURPOSE OF PUNISHMENT

Neither the purpose nor the effect of punishment has ever been definitely agreed upon, even by its most strenuous advocates. So long as punishment persists it will be a subject of discussion and dispute. No doubt the idea of punishment originated in the feeling of resentment and hatred and vengeance that, to some extent at least, is incident to life. The dog is hit with a stick and turns and bites the stick. Animals repel attack and fight their enemies to death. The primitive man vented his hatred and vengeance on things animate and inanimate. In the tribes no injury was satisfied until some member of the offending tribe was killed. In more recent times family feuds have followed down the generations and were not forgotten until the last member of a family was destroyed. Biologically, anger and hatred follow fear and injury, and punishment follows these in turn. Individuals, communities and whole peoples hate and swear vengeance for an injury, real or fancied. Punishments, even to the extent of death, are inflicted where there can be no possible object except revenge. Whether the victim is weak or strong, old or young, sane or insane, makes no difference; men and societies react to injury exactly as animals react.

That vengeance is the moving purpose of punishment is abundantly shown by the religious teachings that shape the ethical ideas of the Western world. The Old Testament abounds in the justification of vengeance. A few quotations amply show the Biblical approval of this doctrine:

Whoso sheddeth man's blood, by man shall his blood be shed. Genesis 9;6.

No expiation can be made for the land for the blood that is shed therein, but by the blood of him that shed it. Numbers 35;33.

Wherefore should the nations [Gentiles] say, Where is their [the Jews'] God? Let the avenging of the blood of thy servants which is shed, be known among the nations in our sight. Psalms 79;10.

The righteous shall rejoice when he seeth the vengeance; he shall wash his feet in the blood of the wicked; so that men shall say, Verily there is a reward for the righteous, verily there is a God that judgeth in the earth. Psalms 58;10.

And I [God] will execute vengeance in anger and wrath upon the nations which hearkened not. Micah 5;15.

All things are cleansed with blood, and apart from the shedding of blood there is no remission. Hebrews 9;22.

For we know him that said, Vengeance belongeth unto me. . . . It is a fearful thing to fall into the hands of the living God. Hebrews 10;30.

True it is often claimed that Jesus repudiated the doctrine of vengeance. The passage of 5th Matthew, 38-30 is often quoted in proof of this assertion—"Ye have heard that it hath been said, an eye for an eye and a tooth for a tooth. But I say unto you, that ye resist not evil, but whosoever shall smite thee on thy right cheek, turn to him the other also." But the gospels and the other books of the New Testament show plainly that non-resistance was not laid down as a rule for the guidance of mankind, but only as a policy by one sect of the Jews and Christians to save themselves from the Romans. The reason for the doctrine was the belief that resistance was hopeless, and that God who had the power would in his own time visit on the oppressors the vengeance that the Jews and Christians were too weak to inflict. Jesus and the early Christians knew of no people beyond their immediate territory, and they did not appeal to mankind as a whole, or to future generations.

The early Christians believed in judging and in punishment as vengeance, the same as the Jews and other peoples believed in it. (See 13 Matthew 41-43, 23 Matthew 33, 25 Matthew 46.) They believed that the end of the world was at hand; that the coming of the Lord was imminent; that some of that generation would not taste death, and that God would punish sinners in his own time. The New Testament is replete with this doctrine, which was stated and elaborated in the so-called " Revelations of St. Peter."

Probably this document was composed about the year 150 A.D. and by the year 200 it was read as " Scripture " in some Christian communities. Subsequently it disappeared and was known only by name until a substantial fragment of the document was discovered at Akhmim in Egypt, in the year 1887. A portion of it represents a scene in which the disciples of Jesus ask him to show them the state of the righteous dead, in order that this knowledge may be used to encourage people to accept Christianity. The request is granted and the disciples are shown not only a vision of the delightful abodes of the righteous, but also a vivid picture of the punishments that are being meted out to the wicked. It is interesting to note how the punishments are devised to balance in truly retributive fashion the crimes mentioned. It is this type of tradition that furnished Dante and Milton the basis for their pictures of hell.

The following is the more interesting portion of this document:

And the Lord showed me [Peter] a very great country outside of this world, exceeding bright with light, and the air there lighted with rays of the sun, and the earth itself blooming with unfading flowers and full of spices and plants, fair-flowering and incorruptible and bearing blessed fruit. And so great was the perfume that it was borne thence even unto us. And the dwellers in that place were clad in the raiment of shining angels and their raiment was like unto their country; and angels hovered about them there. And the glory of the dwellers there was equal, and with one voice they sang praises alternately to the Lord God, rejoicing in that place. The Lord said to us, This is the place of your brethren the righteous.

And over against that place I saw another, exceedingly parched, and it was the place of punishment. And those who were being punished there and the angels who punished them wore dark raiment like the air of the place.

Certain persons there were hanging by the tongue. These were they who blaspheme the way of righteousness, and under them lay a fire whose flames tortured them.

Also there was a great lake full of flaming mire in which were certain men that pervert righteousness, and tormenting angels afflicted them.

And there were also others, women, hanged by their hair over that mire that flamed up, and these were they who adorned themselves for adultery. And the men who mingled with them in the defilement of adultery, were hanging by the feet with their heads in that mire, and they exclaimed in a loud voice: We did not believe that we should come to this place.

And I saw the murderers and their accomplices cast into a certain narrow place full of evil snakes where these evil beasts smote them while they turned to and fro in that punishment, and worms like great black clouds afflicted them. And the souls of those who had been murdered said, as they stood and looked upon the punishment of their murderers, O God, just is thy judgment.

And other men and women were aflame up to the middle, and were cast into a dark place and were beaten by evil spirits, and their inwards were eaten by restless worms. These were they who persecuted the righteous and delivered them up to the authorities.

And over against these were other men and women gnawing their tongues and having flaming fire in their mouths. These were false witnesses.

And in a certain other place there were pebbles sharper than swords or any needle, red hot, and women and men in tattered and filthy raiment, rolled about on them in punishment. These were the rich who trusted in their riches and had no pity for orphans and widows and despised the commandment of God.

And in another great lake full of boiling pitch and blood and mire stood men and women up to their knees. These were the usurers and those who take compound interest.

The noted preacher, scholar and president of Princeton College, Jonathan Edwards, in his famous sermon, "Sinners in the Hands of an Angry God," put in forcible and picturesque language the religious and legal view of punishment as vengeance:

They [sinners] deserve to be cast into hell; so that divine justice never stands in the way, it makes no objection against God's using His power at any moment to destroy them. Yea, on the contrary, justice calls aloud for an infinite punishment on their sins. Divine justice says of the tree that brings forth such grapes of Sodom, "Cut it down, why cumbereth it the ground?" Luke xiii. 7. The sword of divine justice is every moment brandished over their heads, and it is nothing but the hand of arbitrary mercy, and God's mere will, that holds it back.

They are now the objects of that very same anger and wrath of God, that is expressed in the torments of hell: and the reason why they do not go down to hell at each moment, is not because God, in whose power they are, is not then very angry with them; as angry as He is with many of those miserable creatures that He is now tormenting in hell, and do there feel and bear the fierceness of His wrath. Yea, God is a great deal more angry with great numbers that are now on earth; yea, doubtless, with many that are now in this congregation, that, it may be, are at ease and quiet, than He is with many of those that are now in the flames of hell.

So that it is not because God is unmindful of their wickedness and does not resent it, that He does not let loose His hand and cut them off. God is not altogether such a one as themselves, though they imagine Him to be so. The wrath of God burns against them; their damnation does not slumber; the pit is prepared; the fire is made ready; the furnace is now hot; ready to receive them; the flames rage and glow. The glittering sword is whet and held over them, and the pit hath opened her mouth under them.

The God that holds you over the pit of hell, much as one holds a spider, or some loathsome insect over the fire, abhors you, and is dreadfully provoked; His wrath towards you burns like fire; He looks upon you as worthy of nothing else, but to be cast into the fire; He is of purer eyes than to bear to have you in His sight; you are ten thousand times more abominable in His eyes than the most hateful and venomous serpent is in ours. You have offended Him infinitely more than ever a stubborn rebel did his prince: and yet it is nothing but His hand that holds you from falling into the fire every moment; it is ascribed to nothing else, that you did not go to hell the last night; that you was suffered to awake again in this world, after you closed your eyes to sleep; and there is no other reason to be given, why you have not dropped into hell since you arose in the morning, but that God's hand has held you up; there is no other reason to be given why you have not gone to hell, since you have sat here in the house of God provoking His pure eyes by your sinful, wicked manner of attending His solemn worship; yea, there is nothing else that is to be given as a reason why you do not this very moment drop down into hell.

O sinner! consider the fearful danger you are in: it is a great furnace of wrath, a wide and bottomless pit, full of the fire of wrath, that you are held over in the hand of that God whose wrath is provoked and incensed as much against you as against many of the damned in hell: you hang by a slender thread, with the flames of divine wrath flashing about it, and ready every moment to singe it and burn it asunder; and you have no interest in any Mediator, and nothing to lay hold of to save yourself, nothing to keep off the flames of wrath, nothing of your own, nothing that you ever have done, nothing that you can do, to induce God to spare you one moment.

Consider this, you that are here present, that yet remain

in an unregenerate state. That God will execute the fierceness of His anger, implies that He will inflict wrath without any pity.

Even though increasing knowledge may have somewhat softened the language of vengeance, still both religion and the law have found their chief justification for punishment in the doctrine of revenge.

The church has constantly taught from the first that God would punish the sinner with everlasting torment. It has taught that all are bad from birth and can be saved only by grace. The punishment to be suffered was as terrible as man's mind could conceive. It would continue infinitely beyond the time when it might be needed for correction or example. In spite of a few humane or over-sensitive ministers, the doctrine persists and is carefully preserved by the church. That the State likewise holds fast to the idea of vengeance, punishment for the sake of suffering, is just as evident. One needs only to note the force and degree of hatred of the good to the one accused of crime, and the zeal that is shown for a man hunt, to realize how deeply the feeling of vengeance is planted in the structure of man. The truth is that it was a part of life before religion and political institutions were evolved.

Still, most people are now ashamed to admit that punishment is based on vengeance and, for that reason, various excuses and apologies have been offered for the cruelty that goes with it. Some of the more humane, or "squeamish," who still believe in punishment, contend that the object of this infliction is the reformation of the victim. This, of course, cannot be urged of the death penalty or even punishment for life, or for very long-term sentences. In these cases there is neither inducement to reform nor any object in the reformation. No matter how thorough the reform, the prisoner never goes back to society, or he returns after there is no longer a chance for him to be of use to the world or to enjoy life.

Those who say that punishment is for the purpose of reforming the prisoner are not familiar with human psychology. The prison almost invariably tends to brutalize men and breeds bitterness and blank despair. The life of the ordinary prisoner is given over to criticism and resentment against existing things, especially to settled hatred of those who are responsible for his punishment. Only a few, and these are the weakest, ever blame themselves for their situation. Every man of intelligence can trace the various steps that led him to the prison door, and he can feel, if he does not understand, how inevitable each step was. The number of "repeaters" in prison shows the effect of this kind of a living death upon the inmates. To be branded as a criminal and turned out in the world again leaves one weakened in the struggle of life and handicapped in a race that is hard enough for most men at the best. In prison and after leaving prison, the man lives in a world of his own; a world where all moral values are different from those professed by the jailer and society in general. The great influence that helps to keep many men from committing crime — the judgment of his fellows — no longer deters him in his conduct. In fact, every person who understands penal institutions — no matter how well such places are managed — knows that a thousand are injured or utterly destroyed by service in prison, where one is helped.

Very few persons seriously believe that offenders are sent to prison out of kindness to the men. If there were any foundation for this idea, each prisoner would be carefully observed, and when he was fit would be returned to the world. Not even the parole laws, which provide various reasons and ways for shortening sentences, ever lay down the rule that one may be released when he has reformed.

A much larger class of people offers the excuse that punishment deters from crime. In fact, this idea is so well rooted that few think of questioning it. The idea that punishment deters from crime does not mean that the individual prisoner is prevented from another criminal act. A convicted man is kept in jail for as long a time as in the judgment of the jury, the court, or the parole board, will make him atone, or at least suffer sufficiently for the offence. If the terms are not long enough, they can be made longer. The idea that punishment deters, means that unless A shall be punished for murder, then B will kill; therefore A must be punished, not for his own sake, but to keep B from crime. This is vicarious punishment which can hardly appeal to one who is either just or humane. But does punishing A keep B from the commission of crime? It certainly does not make a more social man of B. If it operates on him in any way it is to make him afraid to commit crime; but the direct result of scaring B is not to keep him from the commission of crime, but to make him use precautions that will keep him safe from discovery. How far the fear of detection and punishment prevents crime is, of course, purely theoretical and cannot be settled either by statistics or logic. One thing is sure, that if B is kept from crime, it is through fear, and of all the enemies of man, fear is the one which causes most misery and pain.

There are many facts that show that the punishment of one does not deter others. Over and over again crimes are committed, by the young especially, that resemble in every detail a previous crime which has received large publicity through the newspapers, often through the hanging of some culprit. Even the unthinking public, always clamoring for severe penalties, does not believe that the example of punishment deters. The public forbids the exhibition of pictures of hangings and of crimes. Somehow, vaguely and dimly as most men see everything, the public realizes that instead of punishments preventing crime, punishments suggest crime. In the olden days when men admitted that vengeance and punishment went together, they were at least more logical, for executions were in the open light of day so all might see and be deterred.

But this sort of punishment was abolished long ago. Now executions are behind tightly-closed doors, often before day-break, with no one present but a doctor to pronounce the victim dead, a preacher to try to save his soul, and a few favored guests. The most humane individuals advocate suppressing the stories in the newspapers, beyond an obituary notice for the deceased, and forbidding the publication of the details of the crime and its penalty. So far as this succeeds, it is a confession that punishment does not deter, but instead suggests and encourages crime. The idea that crime is prevented by punishment, if believed, would be followed by requirements that the young should visit prisons that they might realize the consequences of crime, and that all executions should be public and should be performed on the highest hill.

So much has been written about the decrease of crime that follows the reduction of penalties, and likewise about the numerous crimes of violence which generally follow public hangings, that it is hardly necessary to recall it to the reader. The fact is, those who say that punishment deters have no confidence in their own statement.

The operations of the human mind have always been clouded in mystery and obscurity. The effect of what is seen and heard and felt has never been certain. The great power of suggestion, especially with the young, is only now beginning to be understood. Many things can be done by suggestion. The immature brain records everything that the senses carry to it through the nerves; these records, through lively imagination, are constantly suggesting and urging to action. All good teachers and observing parents know its power and, so far as such matters can be proved, it seems clear that the details of crime and punishment reproduce themselves over and over again by the suggestion carried to the mind, especially with the young. There is every reason to think that suggestions of crime will affect the mind as much as suggestions of adventure, love or war.

Does it then follow that no one shall be restrained from freedom on account of either his actions or his nature? It is really idle to ask this question. No matter what one may think of the so-called criminal and his responsibility, or quite regardless of whether we feel pity or hatred, the great mass of the community will not suffer one who has little self-control to interfere seriously and directly with the peace and happiness of the community in which he lives. Whether by the action of the law or by vigilance committees, some men will not be allowed to be at large. Doubtless under proper treatment and environment most of this sort of anti-social conduct would disappear, but for many years to come it will remain.

Taking away the liberty of another has only one justification. The great mass of people in any community must and will act for self-defense. It needs no fine-spun theories to justify it. Hatred should have nothing to do with it. The conduct of man in this regard is only like that of the animal which destroys the one that is inimical to the pack or herd. The self-protection of the group is the same as the self-protection of the individual. Both the group and the man will save their lives against a lunatic or any other menace, regardless of the nature of the menace.

Punishment, in the proper meaning of the term, cannot be justified by any reasoning. Punishment really means the infliction of pain because the individual has wilfully transgressed. Its supposed justification is that somehow the evil done is atoned for, or made good, or balanced if the author of the evil shall suffer pain. Punishment means that the suffering by the victim is the end, and it does not mean that any good will grow out of the suffering. It seems as if the question only needed to be stated for right-thinking men to deny the validity of punishment.

It may be argued that whether the victim is punished or simply restrained can make no difference. In this lies the whole difference between scientific and humane treatment of the unfortunate, and the vengeful punishments that have always been visited by the strong upon the helpless and the weak. Society restrains the imbecile, the dangerously insane, the victims of deadly, contagious diseases. All these are restrained without any feeling of hatred, but with pity and understanding. Society does not keep one of these persons under restraint after he has sufficiently recovered to make it safe to return him to the community; neither does it release one until he is safe. It uses the best methods for his treatment that may make him fit to live with his fellows, and the best efforts to place him in a proper environment when discharged. Neither does any disgrace nor humiliation nor handicap attach to the unfortunate when discharged. In a sense, the attitude of mind held by the group toward the "criminal" is the whole question. From this everything follows, and without it change or humanity or hope is not possible.

It is true that insane asylums, homes for the feeble-minded, and hospitals are not what they should be, nor what they will be some day. All of this is not due to the attitude of the mind of the public, but is due to the method of administration which is not within the scope of this book. If justice and humanity shall ever have to do with the treatment of the criminal, and if science shall ever be called upon in this, one of the most serious and painful questions of the ages, it is necessary, first, that the public shall have a better understanding of crime and criminals.

III

RESPONSIBILITY FOR CRIME

It is only lately that we are beginning to find out anything about the origin and nature of man. Laws have come down to us from old customs and folk-ways based on primitive ideas of man's origin, capacity and responsibility. It has been generally assumed that man was created different from all the rest of animal life; that man alone was endowed with a soul and with the power to tell good from evil; that in the beginning man was perfect but yielded to temptation, and since then has been the subject of an everlasting contest between the powers of light and the powers of darkness for the possession of his soul; that man not only knew good from evil, but was endowed with "free will," and had the power to choose between good and evil; and that when he did wrong he deliberately chose to do so out of an abandoned and malignant heart; and that all men alike were endowed with this power and all alike were responsible for their acts.

The old indictments charged that: "John Smith, being a wicked, malicious and evil disposed person, not having the fear of God before his eyes, but being moved and seduced by the instigation of the devil etc." It followed, of course, that John Smith should be punished or made to suffer, for he had purposely brought all the evil on himself. The old idea is still the foundation of the world's judgment of men, in court and out. Of course this idea leaves no room for mercy and understanding. Neither does it leave any chance to give the criminal the proper treatment for his defects which might permit him to lead a normal life.

As a matter of fact, every scientific man knows that the origin of life is quite different from this; that the whole current conception of the individual and his responsibility is a gross error; and that no correct judgments can be based on the old foundation; that no sane treatment of crime can follow this assumption of man's origin and nature; that the result of this foundation is almost infinite injustice and cruelty to a large and constantly growing number of men and women; and that it tends to endless injury and evil to society. The conception of man and the treatment of crime and criminals by the courts is not better nor more scientific than was the old-time doctors' treatment of physical ailments by magic, incantations and sorcery.

The origin and development of all animal life is the same. In fact, the development of plant life is on a similar pattern. The origin of a human being is a simple cell, an egg. This cell is fertilized and through growth after fertilization begins dividing and building and taking on the form and semblance of a human being. All children have the same origin, the same development and the same pattern, yet no two are alike. Each has a distinct and different equipment from any of the others. The size of the body, real and potential; the size and fineness of the brain; the delicacy and sensitiveness of the nervous system; the innate instincts upon which conduct mainly rests; the emotions which control action and which flow from the structure — in short, the degree of perfection and imperfection of the machine is all hidden in the original cell. No well-informed person now thinks of questioning the fact that the main characteristics of the human being, as of every other animal and plant, are hidden in the germ or seed from which it sprang.

The laws of growth and development which govern organic matter were not made for man and do not except man. Life begins with the cell and evolves according to pattern. If the cell is that of a human being, it will be black or white, male or female, tall or short, intelligent or stupid, sensitive or stolid; it will develop a large or a small brain, a fine one or a poor one, a sensitive nervous system or a defective one; it will be ruled by instincts that are all-powerful and controlling, and even the color of the hair and eyes are in the pattern. The whole structure, potentially, is in the original cell, and infinite knowledge could tell how the structure would respond to sensations as it passed through life.

It is obvious that the kinds and differences of human structures are infinite. It is no more possible for all men to respond equally to the same stimulus, than it is for all machines or all animals to respond alike. It is apparent that not one of the structures can ever work perfectly, and that from the best down to the poorest structures are infinite degrees of perfection, even down to the machine that has no capacity for any kind of work.

No ordinarily intelligent farmer doubts for a moment that all of this is true in the breeding of stock. He would never expect the same results from various breeds of cattle or even from all cattle of the same breed.

There is no exception to the rule that the whole life, with every tendency, is potential in the original cell. An acorn will invariably produce an oak tree. It can produce no other tree, and it will always develop true to its own pattern. The tree may be larger or smaller, more or less symmetrical, stronger or weaker, but always true to the general pattern of the oak. Variations will be certain, due in part to heredity and in part to environment.

That the baby had nothing to do with its equipment will readily be admitted by everyone. The child is born with a brain of a certain size and fineness. It is born with a nervous system made up of an infinite number of fine fibers reaching all parts of the body, with fixed stations or receivers like the central stations of a telephone system, and with a grand central exchange in the brain. If one can imagine all of the telephone wires in the world centered in one station, he may have some sort of a conception of the separate nerves that bring impressions to the brain and send directions out from it, which together make up the nervous system of man. None of these systems is perfect. They are of all degrees of imperfection down to the utterly useless or worse than useless system. These nerves are of all degrees of sensitiveness and accuracy in receiving and transmitting messages. Some may work well, others imperfectly. No one is much surprised when an automobile, equipped with a mechanism much simpler than the nervous system, refuses to respond properly.

The child is born without knowledge but with certain tendencies, instincts, capacities and potential strength or weakness. His nervous system and his brain may be good or bad — most likely neither very good nor very bad. All of his actions both as a child and as a man are induced by stimulation from without. He feels, tastes, sees, hears or smells some object, and his nerves carry the impression to his brain where a more or less correct registration is made. Its correctness depends largely upon the perfection of the nervous system and the fineness of the material on which the registration is made. Perfect or imperfect, the child begins to gather knowledge and it is stored in this way. To the end of his days he receives impressions and stores them in the same manner. All of these impressions are more or less imperfectly received, imperfectly conveyed and imperfectly registered. However, he is obliged to use the machine he has. Not only does the machine register impressions but it sends out directions immediately following these impressions: directions to the organism as to how to run, to walk, to fight, to hide, to eat, to drink, or to make any other response that the particular situation calls for.

Then, too, stimulated by these impressions, certain secretions are instantly emptied from the ductless glands into the blood which, acting like fuel in an engine, generate more power in the machine, fill it with anger or fear and prepare it to respond to the directions to fight or flee, or to any type of action incident to the machine. It is only within a few years that biologists have had any idea of the use of these ductless glands or of their importance in the functions of life. Very often these ductless glands are diseased, and always they are more or less imperfect; but in whatever condition they are, the machine responds to their flow.

The stored-up impressions are more or less awakened under stimulation. As life goes on, these stored impressions act as inhibitions or stimulations to action, as the case may be. These form the material for comparisons and judgments as to conduct. Not only are the impressions imperfect and the record imperfect, but their value and effect depend on the brain which compares and considers the impressions. From all this mechanism, action is born.

That man is the product of heredity and environment and that he acts as his machine responds to outside stimuli and nothing else, seem amply proven by the evolution and history of man. But, quite aside from this, logic and philosophy must lead to the same conclusions. This is not a universe where acts result from chance. Law is everywhere supreme. Every process of nature and life is a continuous sequence of cause and effect. No intelligent person would ever think of an effect in the physical world which did not follow a cause or causes. It has taken man a long time to find this out. The recurrence of the seasons, the seed-time and harvest, the common phenomena of Nature, were once supposed to be outside the realm of cause and effect and due to the whim of some powerful being. But the laws of matter are now coming to be understood. Chance, accident and whim have been banished from the physical world. The acts of men alone are supposed to be outside the realm of law. There is a cause for the eternal revolution of the earth around the sun, for the succession of seed-time and harvest, for growth and decay; but not for the thoughts and actions of man.

All the teaching of the world is based on the theory that there is no free will. Why else should children be trained with so much care? Why should they be taught what is right and what is wrong? Why should so much pains be taken in forming habits? To what effect is the storing of knowledge in the brain of the child, except that it may be taught to avoid the wrong and to do the right? Man's every action is caused by motive. Whether his action is wise or unwise, the motive was at least strong enough to move him. If two or more motives pulled in opposite directions, he could not have acted from the weakest but must have obeyed the strongest. The same motives applied to some other machine might have produced an opposite result, but to his particular structure it was all-controlling. How any special motive will affect any special machine must depend upon the relative strength of the motive and make of the machine. It is for this reason that intelligent people have always taken so much pains to fortify the machine, so that it would respond to what they believed was right. To say that one could ever act from the weakest motive would bring chaos and chance into a world of method and order. Even punishment could have no possible effect to deter the criminal after release, or to influence others by the example of the punishment. As well might the kernel of corn refuse to grow upward to the sunlight, and grow downward instead.

Before any progress can be made in dealing with crime the world must fully realize that crime is only a part of conduct; that each act, criminal or otherwise, follows a cause; that given the same conditions the same result will follow forever and ever; that all punishment for the purpose of causing suffering, or growing out of hatred, is cruel and anti-social; that however much society may feel the need of confining the criminal, it must first of all understand that the act had an all-sufficient cause for which the individual was in no way responsible, and must find the cause of his conduct, and, so far as possible, remove the cause.

IV

ENVIRONMENT

The acorn will inevitably produce the oak tree and it will grow true to its pattern. All seeds and cells will do likewise. Still if the acorn is planted in good soil, where it is properly nourished and in a spot where it is sufficiently sheltered, the tree will be more likely to become large and symmetrical, than if it is planted in poor soil or in an exposed spot.

In one sense heredity is the seed, and environment the soil. The whole structure and pattern and inherent tendencies and potentiality are in the seed and cannot be changed. The child has nothing to do with its early environment during the period when impressions sink the deepest and when habits are formed. It is then that the meaning of facts is interpreted. At this time the child is fashioned by the teachings and environment in which it is placed. As the child receives its first impressions, and all along through its development, it is forming habits from those about it. These habits come to be strong, dominating forces in its life. Very few people, if any, can trace definite views of conduct or thought to their conscious effort, but these are born of their structure and the environment that formed their habits after birth.

The fact that an individual's political and religious faith depends almost entirely on his place of birth and early youth, shows the strength of environment in forming and shaping opinions and beliefs.

As the child grows and develops, it is influenced by all that surrounds it. The human machine moves in response to outside stimulation. How it will move depends upon two things, the character of the stimulant and the machine to which it is applied. No two machines will act exactly alike from the same stimulus. Sometimes they act in diametrically opposite ways. For instance, under the same stimulation, one may run and another may fight, depending perhaps on the secretions that the ductless glands empty into the blood.

No machine can act except according to its make-up. Even an ignorant person, who finds that the same stimulant produces different results on different machines, would know that the structures are not the same.

Endless discussions have been devoted to the relative importance of heredity and environment in human conduct. This is a fruitless task. In a sense, each one is of supreme importance in the outcome of a life. It is obvious that some structures are so perfect that almost no environment will overcome them. Instances of strong men developing out of poor environment are not rare. Many of these may be subject to doubt as to whether the heredity caused the strength, for the smallest particle of luck at some special or vital time may make all the difference possible in the outcome of a life. While some heredities withstand a poor environment, others are so poor that, no matter how good the environment, the machine cannot survive. An idiot is an illustration of one whom environment cannot change. No heredity will overcome the hardest environment. The old saying, "every man has his price," is true in this sense, that every machine will stand just so much and no more. Some machines reach the breaking point soon and some later, but all have their limit. Most people have a heredity that is not the best nor yet the worst. Given an imperfect machine, they are thrown into a certain environment, and then up to the capacity of their machines the outcome depends entirely on the environment. Given an environment easy enough they will succeed, or at least "get by." Given a hard environment they will fail, or "go down." Tens of thousands of men live in a comparatively easy environment and pass their lives as useful citizens with no taint of criminality to their names, who under a hard environment would be found in prison. On the other hand, perhaps most of the inmates of prisons would have lived as respected citizens if their environment had not been so hard. Heredity has everything to do with making the machine strong and capable, or weak and useless; but when the machine is made and thrown on the world in its imperfect shape, environment has everything to do in determining what its fate shall be.

V

ADJUSTING HEREDITY AND ENVIRONMENT

Most people live a narrow existence. Perhaps the great majority of men and women find their safety in this kind of a life. The adjustment of heredity and environment is not an easy task to one who lives an unsheltered life. The ordinary person, thrown on his own resources, is poorly equipped for existence. His opinions on most matters are not sound. He uses poor judgment as to how he shall spend the little money he gets. He is generally driven by debts and harassed in all his efforts to get a living. A large family adds to his trouble and his existence is a constant struggle with what, to him, is an almost hopeless fate.

Industrial conditions for the most part are relentless and hard. The poor man is thrown into competition with his fellows for work. He may get along when work is easy to get and wages are good, but in dull times he falls behind, and is in hopeless trouble. His life is a long, hard struggle to make adjustments to his environment, and it is not strange that he goes down so often before the heavy task. Failure to make proper adjustments directly and indirectly often means prison to him.

Again, the ordinary and especially the weak man is hopelessly puzzled by his environment. It must never be overlooked that man has a lowly origin. The marks of his humble birth are in his whole structure and life. His make-up has been the work of the ages. He is a late development of a life that knew nothing of law, as law is understood today. His ancestors were hungry and went out after food, they killed their prey and took their food by main strength whenever they had the power. They were subject to certain customs which were very strict, but which were few and did not seriously complicate life. They knew only the law of force. Their existence was simple and primal, and they were governed by no " rights," except such simple ones as were made by might and custom.

Civilization is a constant building-up of limitations around heredity; a persistent growth of environmental control as it progresses, or at least moves along. This structure, especially the legal structure, is built by the more intelligent and always by the strong men. It is always shifting and moving, and it is impossible for the inferior man to adjust his emotions and his life rapidly to the changes. Things which are not condemned by his feelings of right and wrong are condemned by laws that meet with no response from his emotions and moral ideas. To him at least these are not different from the things that are done by others with impunity and without rebuke. Especially is this true of the rapidly growing class of property laws that have had no counterpart in the early history of man. This list has grown so fast that it is beyond the power of a large class of men to find in their feelings any response to many of these criminal statutes. The ever-growing social restrictions are of the same modern growth, and it is equally impossible to feel and understand them. What we call civilization has moved so fast that the structure and instincts of man have not been able to become adjusted to it. The structure is too cumbersome, too intense, too hard, and if not breaking down of its own weight, it is at least destroying thousands who cannot adjust themselves to its changing demands. Not only are the effects of this growing body of social and legal restrictions shown directly by their constant violation, generally by the inferior and the poor, but indirectly in their strain on the nervous system; by the irritation and impatience that they generate, and which, under certain conditions cause acts of violence.

VI

PSYCHOLOGY OF CRIMINAL CONDUCT

No one can understand conduct without knowing something of the psychology of human action. First of all, it must be understood that reason, which so many have idealized and placed in control of the human machine, has little to do with the actions of men. It is a common habit with most men to find fault with and bewail the fact that human beings do not act from reason. However much the truth is impressed upon us, we never seem to realize that the basis of action is in instinct and emotion. It is really useless to quarrel with Nature. Whether it would have been better to have made man some other way is not worth discussing. He has been evolved in a certain way and we must take him as he is. Our impatience with the method that Nature has provided for influencing human conduct is largely due to our idea of the meaning of life.

Man has fancied himself in a position in the animal world that facts of life and nature do not sustain. We seem to feel that man has some high calling; that he should make something of himself which cannot be accomplished; that he should form some sort of a perfect order that he never can reach; in short that man has a purpose and a mission. It is manifest that all we know is but a mite compared with the unknown, and it may be that sometime a purpose will be revealed of which man never dreamed. Still from all that we can see and understand, Nature has but one desire, and that is the preservation and perpetuation of life. This is its purpose or, rather, its strongest urge not only with men but with all animal life. Sometimes to create one fish a million eggs are spawned. Nature is profligate both in spawning life and compassing its destruction. In the human species the capacity for life is immeasurably beyond its fruition. A large portion of those who are born die an early death. And that human life shall not be extinct, Nature plants the life-giving desire deep in the constitution of man. The creation of life comes from an instinct so profound and absorbing that it carries a train of evils in its wake. Many are overweighted by the sex instinct to their positive harm. Nature somehow did not trust such a fundamental duty as the preservation of the race to reason. If intellectual processes were responsible for life, the world no doubt would soon be bare of animate things. Neither could the care of the young be trusted to anything but the deep-seated instinct that causes the mother to forget her own life in the preservation of the life of her child.

The functions of body, on which life is founded, do not depend upon reason. The heart begins to beat before birth; it continues to beat until the end of life. The reason has nothing to do with the heart performing its function. Man goes to sleep at night confident that it will still be beating in the morning. The blood circulates in the veins independent of the thoughts of man. The digestive processes go on whether he sleeps or is awake. Many of his muscles never rest from birth to death. Life could not be preserved through the intellectual processes.

Human action is governed largely by instinct and emotion. These instincts and emotions are incident to every living machine and are the motor forces that impel the organism. They do not think. They act, and act at once. All the mind can do is to place some restraint on such instincts and emotions through experience, education and settled habits. If the actions are never inhibited, the machine will tear itself to pieces. If too easily inhibited, it will do no work. It is manifest that the perfect machine does not exist.

Man is moved by his instinct of flight and his emotion of fear, which are set in motion by apprehended dangers and by unaccustomed sights or sounds. Terror sometimes becomes so intense that it prevents flight and brings convulsions and death. It is idle to reason with one in terror. It is idle to reason with a mob in terror or a nation in terror. One might as well expect to calm a tempestuous sea with soft words.

The instinct of repulsion brings hatred and dislike and, combined with the instinct of pugnacity, may lead to crimes of violence. When these instincts are strong enough, the weak and superficial barriers cannot stand against them. An electrical flash showing the scaffold with the noose above it would have no force to stop an instinct and emotion fully aroused. Through seeing, feeling, hearing, tasting or smelling, some instinct is called into action. Many times several conflicting instincts are aroused. The man is like a tree bent back and forth by the storm. If the storm is hard enough, sooner or later it will break. Which way the tree falls has nothing to do with the consciousness of the tree, but has to do only with the direction of the prevailing and controlling force.

The instinct of gregariousness draws animals or men together into communities and close relations. This is one of the strongest instincts and not only preserves life but is fundamental to those human associations that are the basis of civilization. Except for this, animals would live a lonely life and probably perish from the earth. Through this instinct, man builds his villages and cities and organizes his states and nations. With the gregarious instinct and the parental instinct drawing men together, and the instincts and emotions of flight, fear and pugnacity, repelling and pushing them apart, conflict is inevitable. All that can be done is to create and cultivate as strong habits, customs and laws as possible to stand against the power of instinct and emotion in time of need, and to remove the main inciting causes so far as man has the intelligence and power to remove them. It is evident that this can never be complete. There are too many weak machines, too many defective nervous systems, too many badly organized brains. Accidents are inevitable, and some accidents are called "crimes." When the accident is international or world-wide, it means war. Those who believe that there is any power to stop all the harmful manifestations of man's instincts, either individually or *en masse,* do not understand the fundamental nature of man.

Many and probably all instincts work both for good and ill. Flight, pugnacity, repulsion, sex — all are life-preserving or life-destroying, as the case may be. A certain degree of excitation brings life and pleasure. A stronger or weaker may bring calamity and death. The parental instinct, with the instinct of reproduction, is fundamental to life.

It is the basis of tenderness and sympathy, and is likewise the foundation of jealousy and often of hatred and pugnacity. At one time it may mean the deepest and most abiding pleasures of life, and at another it may bring death. Life cannot exist without it, and yet, that it may persist, Nature seriously overloads many machines with disastrous results. History is replete with the helplessness of reason and judgment in dealing with these emotions. Neither when they act for good nor for ill can reason and judgment have the slightest weight when these instincts and emotions are stirred to the depths.

The emotion to acquire and keep property is very strong and perhaps at the base of the deep desire for wealth. This emotion is probably of a comparatively late growth, but today it seems to have taken its place as one of the strongest that move men. This emotion, like all others, prompts man to get what he wants. It of course does not suggest the way, but is simply an urge to acquire and possess. It is modified and hedged about by customs and habits but, like all instincts, its strength is always seeking ways to accomplish results regardless of the rules laid down and thus urging their violation. With weak machines and imperfect systems, where not only are the restrictions imperfect, the habits not well defined, but where it is impossible to satisfy the instinct under the rules laid down, there can be but one result; a large number will take property wherever and however they can get it.

The instinct for acquisition is so strong that men are constantly contriving new and improved methods for getting property. Often the new methods come under restraint of the law. The enactment of the law does not give man the feeling that a thing is wrong which before was right, and many continue their ways of getting property, regardless of the law. The instinct is too strong, the needs too great, and the barriers too weak.

Instincts are primal to man. He has inherited them from the animal world. Their strength and weakness depend on the make-up of the machine. Some are very strong and some abnormally weak, and there are no two machines that emphasize or repress the same instincts to the same degree. One need but look at his family and neighbors to see the various manifestations of these instincts. Some are quarrelsome and combative and will fight on the slightest provocation. Others are distinctively social; the gregarious instinct is pronounced in many people. These are always seen in company and cannot be alone. They readily adapt themselves to any sort of associations. Others are solitary. They choose to be alone. They shrink from and avoid the society of others. In some the instinct at the basis of sex association is over-strong; they like children; they are generally sympathetic and emotional, and the strength of the instinct often leads them to excesses. Others are entirely lacking in this instinct; they neither care for children nor want them; they habitually avoid association with the other sex. The difference is constituent in the elements that make up the machine.

Everyone is familiar with the varying strength and weakness of the instincts of getting and hoarding as shown by his neighbors and acquaintances. Some seem to have no ambition or thought for getting or keeping money. Some can get it but cannot keep it. Some have in them from childhood the instinct for getting the better of every trade; for hoarding what they get, and accumulating property all their lives. In this, as in all other respects, no two individuals are alike. History is filled with examples of men who had the instinctive power of getting money combined with the instinct for keeping it. Their names are familiar, all the way from Midas and Crœsus down to the prominent captains of industry today. It is common for them and their adherents who criticise new schemes of social organization to remark with the greatest assurance that before wealth can be equal, brains must be equal. The truth is that brains have little to do with either the making or accumulating of money. This depends mainly, like all other activities, on the strength or weakness of the instincts involved. One's brain capacity cannot be measured by his bank account, any more than by the strength of his body or the color of his hair. His bank account simply shows his innate tendencies. There is no doubt that brain capacity as well as physical perfection adds to power, but it is the instinct that determines the tendency and strength of the activity.

To say that the one who gets money the most easily and keeps it the most safely has the best brain is no more reasonable than to say that the foxhound is more intelligent than the bull-dog because it can run faster. Nature formed one for running and the other for holding on. The brain power is not involved.

There are manifold ways of gratifying all these instincts. The desire for property calls simply for getting it and keeping it. It does not involve the method to be used. The way is determined by other faculties, by education, by opportunities, by the strength and weakness of inhibitions. It does not follow that all legal ways are morally right and all illegal ones morally wrong. Society in its development has established certain ways in which it may be done. These ways are easy for some, they are hard for others, and for many quite impossible.

Still the instinct for getting is always present,

leading and urging to acquire and to keep. Endless are the ways that men have contrived to gratify this instinct. If, perchance, a law stands in the way, means are always sought to get around the law. Every desire is always seeking its own gratification or satisfaction. This means life. Most men believe that the way they adopt for getting money or gratifying other instincts is really no worse than some other person's way. The man who uses the confidence game contends with great assurance that his methods are like other business methods; that all men are using every means to get the largest return for the least effort, and one way is no better than another. A considerable portion of society has always supported him in these ideas. The law is full of shadowy lines which divide legal acquisition from the illegal, some of which are so fine that no one can see more than a technical difference. For instance, under an indictment for obtaining money by false pretenses, one may make all sorts of statements as to the quality, value, style and desirability of the article sold, if he does not make a specific statement of a fact regarding the material contained in them or the amount, number, quality or the like. He may lie, but to be safe he must know the kind of lie the law permits. Many lies pass as "puffing goods" and are within the pale. A trader is not expected to tell the truth. What he can and cannot say may be determined only by a careful examination of the law, and not always then.

Infinite are the reasons men give for doing the things that their instincts bid them do. All depends upon the strength of the instinct and the character of the machine; the restrictions and habits formed; and many other factors of which the man knows nothing. In fact, all depends upon his endowment and the outside forces that move to action, and for none of these is he in any way to be praised or blamed.

Society seems to be almost oblivious to the emotional life of man. The great masses of men have no capacity or chance to prepare a proper environment in the intense commercialism and mad rush of today. The laws of trade and commerce give most men food, clothing and shelter but nothing more. There is no beauty in their homes or surroundings; no music or art; no adventure or speculation. Existence is a dead thing, a dreary round. To many such people crime furnishes the only chance for adventure. Take away emotions and life is hopelessly dull and commonplace. The emotions of men must be fed just as the body must be fed. To many religion has furnished this emotional life. Churches have provided some art and some music. But aside from the Catholic Church almost none of this is for the poor. To many if not most people religion cannot take the place of joy. Dogma and creed deaden and cannot appeal to the reason of man. Still they have furnished a large part of the emotional life to great masses of men, without which existence would hold no hope or joy. But this is not enough to fill most lives. The element of joy is largely lacking. To many it makes no appeal, although music and art and beauty do. In no country has society so utterly neglected and ignored the emotional side of man as in America. This has led many men to a life of adventure that for them has been possible only in crime. Many others found this life in the saloon, mixed with influences not conducive to a normal life. The closing of the saloons has added to the already serious need of providing for the innate feelings of men. This is all the more important for America, as a large part of our population has come from lands where beauty and art and music have for generations been made a part of the common life of all.

VII

THE CRIMINAL

Those who have had no experience in the courts and no knowledge of what is known as the "criminal class" have a general idea that a criminal is not like other men. The people they know are law-abiding, conventional believers in the State and the Church and all social customs and relations; they have strict ideas of property rights, and regard the law as sacred. True they have no more acquaintance with law-makers and politicians in general than with the criminal class, which, of course, is one reason why they have such unbounded confidence in the law. Such persons are surprised and shocked when some member of the family or some friend is entangled in the courts, and generally regard it as a catastrophe that has come upon him by accident or a terrible mistake. As a rule, they do all in their power to help him whether he is acquitted or convicted. They never think that he and everyone else they know is not materially different from the ordinary criminal. As a matter of fact, the potential criminal is in every man, and no one was ever so abandoned that some friend would not plead for him, or that some one who knew him would not testify to his good deeds.

The criminal is not hard to understand. He is one who, from inherited defects or from great misfortune or especially hard circumstances, is not able to make the necessary adjustments to fit him to his environment. Seldom is he a man of average intelligence, unless he belongs to a certain class that will be discussed later. Almost always he is below the normal of intelligence and in perhaps half of the cases very much below. Nearly always he is a person of practically no education and no property. One who has given attention to the subject of crime knows exactly where the criminal comes from and how he will develop. The crimes of violence and murder, and the lesser crimes against property, practically all come from those who have been reared in the poor and congested districts of cities and large villages. The robbers, burglars, pickpockets and thieves are from these surroundings. In a broad sense, some criminals are born and some are made. Nearly all of them are both born and made. This does not mean that criminality can be inherited, or even that there is a criminal type. It means that with certain physical and mental imperfections and with certain environment the criminal will be the result.

Seldom does one begin a criminal life as a full-grown man. The origin of the typical criminal is an imperfect child, suffering from some defect. Usually he was born with a weak intellect, or an unstable nervous system. He comes from poor parents. Often one or both of these died or met misfortune while he was young. He comes from the crowded part of a poor district. He has had little chance to go to school and could not have been a scholar, no matter how regularly he attended school. Some useful things he could have learned had society furnished the right teachers, surroundings and opportunities to make the most of an imperfect child. Early in life he does some desultory work in casual occupations. This of course is not steady, but he picks up what he can and keeps the job for a short time, sometimes quitting work because he is discharged and sometimes because, like most boys and men, he does not like to work. His playground is the street, the railroad yards or vacant lots too small for real play, and fit only for a loafing place for boys like himself. These gather nightly and talk of the incidents that interest most people, mainly the abnormal things of life and generally the crimes that the newspapers make so prominent to satisfy the public demand. He learns to go into vacant buildings, steals the plumbing, and he early learns where to sell it. From this it is only a short step to visiting occupied buildings at night. In this way he learns to be a burglar as other boys learn to play baseball or golf.

Naturally he has no strong sense of property rights. He has always had a hard time to get enough to eat and wear, and he has grown up unconsciously to see the inequality of distribution and to believe that it is not fair and that there is little or no justice in the world. As a child he learned to get things the best way he could, and to think nothing about it. In short, his life, like all other lives, moves along the lines of least resistance. He soon comes to feel that the police are his natural enemies and his chief business is to keep from getting caught. Inevitably he is brought into the Juvenile Court. He may be reprimanded at first. He comes again and is placed on probation. The next time he goes to a Juvenile Prison where he can learn all the things he has not found out before. He is known to the police, known to the Court, known to the neighbors. His status is fixed. When released from prison, he takes his old heredity back into his old environment. It is the easiest to him, for he has learned to make his adjustments to this environment. From fifteen to twenty-five years of age, he has the added burden of adolescence, the trying time in a boy's life when sex feelings are developing, when he is passing from childhood to manhood. This is a very difficult time at best to the type of boy from which a criminal grows; he meets it without preparation or instruction. What he knows he learns from others like himself. He gets weird, fantastic, neurotic ideas, which only add to his natural wonderment.

Every person who has not inherited property must live by some trade or calling. Very few people in jail or out choose their profession. Even if one selects his profession it does not follow that he has chosen the calling for which he is best adapted. So far as a person can and does follow his desires, he generally means to choose the calling which will bring him the greatest amount of return for the least exertion. He may have strong inclinations in certain directions, as, for instance, to paint or to write or to investigate or to philosophize, but, as a rule, he does not make his living from following these ambitions. If he does, it is generally a poor living. But usually his aim is to make money at something else so that he can give free rein to his real ambitions.

Most men start to make a living as boys from the ages of fifteen to eighteen. They have no idea of what they ought to do or even of what they want to do. Usually, so far as they have an ambition, it is to do something more or less spectacular that seems to have an element of adventure and not too disagreeable or hard; something like the work of a policeman, a chauffeur, or an employee in a garage. Still, first and last, most boys and most men have no opportunity for choosing an occupation. In fact, the boy is told that he is a man and must get a job long before he knows that he is a man or begins to feel responsibilities, while he still has all the emotions and dreams of a boy.

When he is told he must go to work he looks for a job. He does not wait until he can find the one that fits him. He cannot afford to wait and if he could, he does not know what job would fit. He takes automatically the first place he can get, hoping to find a better one, which generally means an easier one, before very long. It is hard for a boy to stick to work; too many things are calling him away. Every instinct and emotion is urging him to play. New feelings and desires are coaxing him from work. His companions and the boy life in which he has a place urge him to leave his task. Usually he keeps his job no longer than he can help and later looks for something else. The chances are great that he will never find what he wants; that he has not had the preparation or training for a successful workingman's career, whatever that might be. He is a doer of odd jobs and of poorly paid work all his life.

He must have some calling and takes the easiest one, which is often a life of crime. From this start comes the professional criminal so-called. He may make a business of picking pockets. If this comes to be his trade it is very hard for him to give it up. There is so strong an element of chance—he never knows what a pocket will contain — it gratifies a spirit of adventure. Then it is easy. The wages are much greater than he could get in any other calling; the hours are short and it never interferes with his amusements. It is not so dangerous as being a burglar or a switchman, for he can find an excuse for jostling one in the street-cars or in a crowd and thus reaching into a pocket.

The burglar is not so apt to be a professional; his is a bolder and more hazardous trade; if he is caught he is taken from his occupation for a longer time. The great hazard involved in this trade and also the physical strength and fitness of those who follow it lead to its abandonment more frequently than is the case with a pickpocket or a petty thief. Robbery is seldom a profession. It is usually the crime of the young and venturesome and almost surely leads to early disaster. Murder, of course, is never a profession. In a broad way it is the result of accident or passion, or of relations which are too hard to endure.

In prison and out, I have talked with scores of these men and boys. I am sure they rarely tried to deceive me. I have very seldom seen one who felt that he had done wrong, or had any thought of what the world calls reformation. A very few have used the current language of those who talk of reform, but generally they were the weakest and most hopeless of the lot and usually adopted this attitude to deceive. In almost every instance where you meet any sign of intelligence, excuses and explanations are freely made, and these explanations fully justify their points of view. Often too they tell you in sincerity that they believe their way of life is too hard and does not pay; that while they cannot see how they could have done any differently in the past, they believe their experience has taught them to stick by the rules of the game.

The boy delinquent grows naturally and almost inevitably into the man criminal. He has generally never learned a trade. No habits have been formed in his youth to keep him from crime. A life of crime is the only one open to him, and for this life he has had ample experience, inclination and opportunity. Then too for this kind of young man the life of a criminal has a strong appeal. Life without opportunity and without a gambler's chance to win a considerable prize is not attractive to anyone. The conventional man who devotes his life to business or to a profession always has before him the prizes of success — to some honor and glory, and to most of them wealth. Imagine the number of lawyers, doctors and business men who could stick to a narrow path if they knew that life offered no opportunity but drudgery and poverty! Nearly all of these look forward to the prizes of success. Most of them expect success and many get it. For the man that I have described, a life of toil offers no chance of success. His capacity, education and environment deny him the gambler's chance of a prize. As an honest man, he may raise a family, always be in debt, live a life of poverty and hardship and see nothing ahead but drudgery and defeat. This is why so many mediocre men are found in the mountains and oil fields prospecting for hidden wealth. With the chance of a fortune just before them, and no other opportunity to win, they spend their lives without a family or home, urged on by the hope of luck.

The man grown from boyhood into ways of vice and crime sees this hope and this hope only to make a strike. He has no strong convictions and no well-settled habits to hold him back. The fear of the law only means greater caution, and after all he has nothing to lose. In his world arrest and conviction do not mean loss of caste; they mean only bad luck. With large numbers of men crime becomes a trade. It grows to be a business as naturally as any other calling comes to be a trade.

There are other criminals who do not come from the class I have described, but the habitual visitor to criminal courts knows that they are very few.

Of the others, some are born of parents who could care for them and have done their best and yet, in spite of this, they have repeatedly been entangled in the law; these are often the only ones of a large family who have not lived according to the rules of the game. They are different from the other members of the family. For the most part they have some specific congenital defect, or an unstable system that prevents the correct registration of the experiences that produce safe habits, or makes them unable to withstand temptation or suggestion.

Everyone knows how easy it is, especially for children, to react to suggestion. The whole life of a child is a response to suggestion. This is about all there is to education. Even older men constantly and readily yield to suggestion. The results gained by quack doctors, lightning-rod agents, promoters and dealers in oil stocks, mining stocks and an endless number of other stocks, show that the right kind of suggestion is bound to produce results. The dressing of the windows of department stores and the writing of catchy advertisements are a constant recognition of the power of suggestion. So well known is this weakness of human character that schools of salesmanship are regularly organized and promoted to teach the art of getting victims to part with money for things they do not want or need.

Every right-feeling person does everything in his power to educate the child. He is ever watchful through the child's youth and early manhood to equip him with the capacity to make a living. He seeks to build up around him and within him the strongest kind of habits and beliefs. He carefully teaches the child that the only way to live is to observe all the rules laid down by experience and custom, so that he may not react to the temptations that life holds out at every step. Every wise person feels almost certain that if his children are reared without education, without discipline, without training or opportunities, they will almost inevitably swell the ranks of the criminal classes. And it is especially certain that if one of his children is defective or has an unstable nervous system, such a child should never be left without protection and care.

There are professional criminals of a different grade, like the forger and the confidence man. Both of these have generally had some education and a fair degree of intelligence, and have had some advantages in life. The forger, as a rule, is a bookkeeper or an accountant who grows expert with the pen. He works for a small salary and sees nothing better. He grows familiar with signatures. Sometimes he is a clerk in a bank and has the opportunity to study signatures; he begins to imitate them, often with no thought of forging paper. He does it because it is an art and probably the only thing he can do well. Perhaps some hard luck or an unfortunate venture on the Board of Trade, or in a faro bank, makes him write a check or note. He easily convinces himself that he is not getting the salary he earns and that less worthy men prosper while he is poor. Then too his business calls for better clothes and better surroundings than those of the workingman, and gives him many glimpses of easy lives. For a time he may escape. If the amount is not too large it is often passed by without an effort to detect. Sometimes it escapes notice altogether. Some business men write so many checks that they take no pains at the end of the month to figure up their account and examine every check, and never notice it unless the balance given by the bank is so far out of the way that it attracts attention. After a forger grows to be an expert, he can move from town to town. If he is taken and put in prison and finally released, he is hard to cure. Forgery is too easy and he knows of no other trade so good. A large percentage of these men never would have forged, had their wages been higher. Many others are the victims of the get-rich-quick disease; they haunt the gambling houses, brokers' offices and the like. Often when they begin they expect to make the check good; generally, they would have made good if the right card had only turned up in the faro bank, or the right quotation on the stock exchange.

There is another class of forgers, generally bankers, who speculate with trust funds. To cover up the shortage they sign notes expecting that they will never be presented and will deceive no one but the bank examiner. If luck goes against them too long, the bank fails and the forgery is discovered. These are really not forgers, as they never intend to get money on the note. It is only a part of a means to cover up the use of trust funds. Of course, these men are never professional forgers, and are much more apt to die from suicide or a broken heart than to repeat.

But with few exceptions, the criminal comes from the walks of the poor and has no education or next to none. For this society is much to blame. Sometimes he is obliged to go to work too soon, but often he cannot learn at school. This is not entirely the fault of the boy's heredity; it is largely the fault of the school. A certain course of study has been laid out. With only slight changes this course has come down from the past and is fixed and formal. Much of it might be of value to a professional man, but most of it is of no value to the man in other walks of life. Because a boy cannot learn arithmetic, grammar or geography, or not even learn to read and write, it does not follow that he cannot learn at all. He may possibly have marked mechanical ability; he may have more than the ordinary powers of adaptation to many kinds of work. These he could be taught to do and often to do well. Under proper instruction he might become greatly interested in some kind of work, and in the study to prepare him for the work. Then too it is more or less misleading to say that an uneducated man commits crime because he is uneducated. Often his lack of education as well as his crime comes from poverty. Crime and poverty may come from something else. All come because he had a poor make-up or an insufficient chance.

After all, the great majority of men must do some kind of manual labor. Until the time shall come when this kind of work is as easy and as well paid as other employment, no one will do manual labor if he can do any other kind. Perhaps the time may come when the hardest and most disagreeable work will be the best paid. There are too many unskilled workers in proportion to the population to make this seem very near. In the meantime — and that is doubtless a long time — some one must do this work. Much of it is done under supervision and requires no great skill and need not be very disagreeable or hard. In a complex civilization there is room for everyone to contribute to the whole. If our schools are some day what they should be, a large part of their time, in some cases all of it, will be devoted to manual training and will be given to producing skilled workmen. This sort of school work can be made attractive to thousands of boys who can do nothing else. And if easier conditions of life under fairer social surroundings could be added to this kind of education, most boys who now drift into crime would doubtless find the conventional life more profitable and attractive.

VIII

THE FEMALE CRIMINAL

Women furnish only one-fifth to one-tenth of the population of penal institutions. Probably the percentage would be still lower if among these were not a number of rather common convictions for acts which are peculiar to women, like abortion, infanticide, child abandonment and the like. As to the other crimes, few women are burglars or robbers, or guilty of other crimes of violence, except murder. Women steal and poison and blackmail and extort money and lie and slander and gossip, and probably cause as much unhappiness as men; but their crimes, like their lives, are not on so large or adventurous a scale. They do not so readily take a chance; they lack the imagination that makes big criminals or lays broad schemes. In many of their crimes they are often the accomplices of men and take rather a minor part, although sometimes a quite important one. For this reason they are often not detected and frequently not prosecuted, a fact which leaves the percentage smaller than it otherwise would be.

Then too, juries are apt to acquit women of crime even when they are indicted and tried. It must be a positive case and one which calls for no possible feeling of sympathy or where there is no personal appeal that will work the conviction of a woman. Men have so long adopted an attitude of chivalry toward women that very few juries will convict them. This too has much to do with the small number of female convicts.

Some writers claim that the small number of women in penal institutions shows that women are better than men; but this is a hasty conclusion arrived at from insufficient facts. There are fewer female prisoners because women have lived a more protected life; they have not been engaged so generally in business; they have not been so constantly obliged to fight their way in the world; their lives have been more quiet and smooth; they have been surrounded by strong conventions and closely watched. Especially is this true with regard to the girl as compared with the boy. Such protection naturally keeps them from the commission of crime. The great consideration shown to them by prosecuting witnesses, prosecuting officers, judges and juries, supplements the protected life and is an added reason for the showing made by statistics. It is notorious that a woman is seldom convicted of murder. This has been the subject of much complaint on the part of the public; still a man may condemn such acquittals and when placed on a jury will himself vote for acquittal.

After all, the juries are right. Most of the cases of murder against women involve sex relations. Nature has made the bearing and rearing of children first of all the woman's part, and this fact so dominates her life that nothing else seems important to her in comparison. She is not able to judge in a broad and scientific way matters so clearly affecting life. It may even be possible that in the evolution and preservation of life, her judgments are right. At least they are the natural judgments for a large number of women, or these tragedies would not occur. No doubt as woman enters the field of industry formerly monopolized by man, and as she takes her part in politics and sits on juries, the percentage of female criminals will rapidly increase. In fact, the percentage of women prisoners has been climbing for many years. As she takes her place with men she will be more and more judged as men are judged, and will commit the crimes that men commit, and perhaps furnish her fair quota to the penitentiaries and jails.

Whether this will be better or worse for the race is no part of the discussion, and can only be told by long experience. Women must accept the facts and make their choice of activities in view of these facts. Quite apart from any sentiment, I think that it is a mistake to believe that men and women should be judged alike. The structure and nervous system of women cause physical and mental disturbances which affect their judgment and life. If there were any justice in human judgment and civilization, then each human being would be judged according to his make-up, his tendencies, his inclinations and his capacities, and no two would be judged alike.

Any sudden change in the treatment of women in the courts will work a great injustice that will leave its effect on both women and men, and still more on the life of the race.

IX

JUVENILE CRIMINALS

This subject would scarcely have been noted a few years ago. True, there was in the past a small mixture of children in the grist ground out in the criminal courts. Usually they received some leniency, and were viewed with more curiosity than alarm. The juvenile criminal was regarded as a prodigy with a capacity for crimes far beyond his years. Something of the attitude obtained in regard to him which attaches to the child chess player or the child mathematician. The child criminal is now common, and for the most part is a product of the city.

All crime is doubtless much more common in the city than the country, and the young criminal especially is a product of the crowded community. To those who look for natural causes for all phenomena the reason is not far to seek. The city itself is an abnormal thing. Primitive man and his ancestors were never huddled together in great multitudes, as are the dwellers in cities today. To a degree almost all animals are gregarious, but the units of organization are much smaller with them than with man, excepting possibly in the case of the ant and the bee, insects which seem specially adapted to live a highly automatic and coöperative life, such as human beings cannot possibly reach. But primitive men and their direct ancestors lived in small groups. They could not have preserved their life in any other way. They lived by fishing and hunting and by gathering roots, berries and herbs. Later they tended their flocks and cultivated the fields in a simple way.

With the introduction of the modern machine, the factory system and the railroads, in the last century, our great modern cities were evolved. As they grew more complicated, new problems arose. The life of the crowded city is most difficult even for normal men and women. The adjustments are too numerous and too complex for an animal made with simple tastes and for a pastoral life. But, if it is hard for men, it is almost hopeless for children, especially the children of the poor who fill our prisons, asylums and almshouses.

Every child needs the open air and the open life of the country. He needs, first of all, exercise which should be in the form of outdoor play. No healthy boy wants to live indoors, even though his home may be a convenient city "flat." The woods, the fields, the streams, the lakes, the wide common with plenty of room, have always made their natural appeal to the young. And as sunlight kills most of the deadly germs, so outdoor life with exercise and play takes care of most of the unhealthy thoughts, habits and ideas of child-life. In the past, our schools both in the city and country have done little to help the young. For the most part healthy children have always looked on them more or less as prisons. Here they have been confined and kept from exercise and play, to study useless and unrelated facts and to commit to memory dry rules which are forgotten as soon as their minds are ready to retain anything worth while.

Schools should be made to fit the needs of children, and not children to fit schools. The school that does not provide work and play for the child which he is glad to do, has learned little of the psychology and needs of youth. Botany, Zoölogy, Geology and even Chemistry can be taught to children before they learn to read, and taught so that it will seem like play, and through this the pupil will acquire a natural taste for books. It is only within the last few years that the modern school has really begun to educate the child. It has been a hard fight that scientific teachers have waged with conventional education for the right of the child. What has been done is too recent and scattering to show material results.

Nothing is so important to the child as education. The early life is the time that character is formed, habits are made, rules of conduct taught, and it is almost impossible to up-root old habits and inhibitions and implant new ones in later years.

It is true that " the child is father to the man," and he is the father of the criminal as well as the useful citizen. Outside of the hopelessly defective, or those who have very imperfect nervous or physical systems, there is no reason why a child who has had proper mental and physical training and any fair opportunity in life should ever be a criminal. Even most of the mentally defective and those suffering from imperfect nervous systems could be useful to society in a sheltered environment. Poor as the country schools have always been, the outdoor life of the country child is still so great an influence that he generally escapes disaster. He is not sent to a factory, but lives in a small community where he has fresh air and exercise.

Of course here as everywhere we must allow for the defective, the imperfect, the subnormals and the children of the very poor. These unfortunates furnish a large percentage of the inmates of prison, and most of the victims for the scaffold which civilization so fondly preserves.

The growth of the big cities has produced the child criminal. He is clearly marked and well defined. He is often subnormal even down to idiocy. In most cases he is the result of heredity.

Many times he may have fair intelligence, but this is usually attached to an unstable, defective nervous system that cannot do its proper work, and he has had no expert treatment and attention. He is always poor. Generally he has lost one or both parents in youth and has lived in the crowded districts where the home was congested. He has no adequate playground and he runs the streets or vacant, waste places. He associates and combines with others of his kind. He cannot or does not go to school. If he goes to school, he dreads to go and cannot learn the lessons in the books. He likes to loaf, just as all children like to play. He is often set to work. He has no trade and little capacity for skilled work that brings good wages and steady employment. He works no more than he needs to work. Every night and all the days that he can get are spent in idleness on the street with his "gang." He seldom reads books. He lacks the taste for books, and such teachers as he knew had not the wit to cultivate a taste for good reading. Such books as he gets only add to his unhealthy thoughts.

Many writers have classified the crimes that the boy commits. It is scarcely worth the while. He learns to steal or becomes a burglar largely for the love of adventure; he robs because it is exciting and may bring large returns. In his excursions to pilfer property he may kill, and then for the first time the State discovers that there is such a boy and sets in action the machinery to take his life. The city quite probably has given him a casual notice by arresting him a number of times and sending him to a juvenile prison, but it has rarely extended a hand to help him. Any man or woman who has fairly normal faculties, and can reason from cause to effect, knows that the crimes of children are really the crimes of the State and society which by neglect and active participation have made him what he is. When it is remembered that the man is the child grown up, it is equally easy to understand the adult prisoner.

X

HOMICIDE

Crimes against persons are not always as easy to classify and understand as crimes against property. These acts are so numerous and come from so many different emotions and motives, that often the cause is obscure and the explanation not easy to find. Still here, as everywhere in Nature, nothing can happen without a cause, and even where limited knowledge does its best and cannot find causes, our recognition of the connection between cause and effect and the all-inclusiveness of law can leave no doubt that complete knowledge would bring complete understanding.

It is always to be borne in mind in considering this class of crimes that the motive power of life is not reason but instinct. If men lived by reason the race would not survive. The primal things that preserve the race, the hunger for food, drink, sex, are instinctive and not only are not awakened or satisfied by reason, but oftentimes in violation of it. Nature, first of all, sees to the preservation of the species, and acts in a broad way that life may not perish. Nature knows nothing about right and wrong in the sense in which man uses these words. All of our moral conceptions are purely of social origin and hence not instinctive in human life, and are forever giving way to the instincts on which Nature depends. The preservation of life has called for the emotions of hate, fear and love, among the other emotions that move men. The animal fears danger and runs away, and thus life is preserved. The weaker animal is almost entirely dependent for life upon his fear. He is sometimes afraid when there is no danger, but without fear he would be destroyed. Sometimes the animal hates and kills and thus preserves himself. The love of offspring is the cause of the care bestowed upon it which preserves its life. The herd instinct in animal species develops packs and clans and tribes and states. Man is the heir to all the past, and the instincts and emotions of the primitive animal are strong in his being. These may have been strengthened or diluted as the ages have come and gone, but the same instincts furnish the motive power for all his acts. Man fears and hates, and runs or kills and saves his life. He loves, and preserves his offspring.

Man sees an object. Instinctively he may fear it or he may hate it. He may run from it or destroy it. He gathers impressions through his senses. The nerves carry them to the brain. He comes to fear certain persons and things, to hate certain other persons or things, and to love still others. If the hatred is strong enough or the danger great enough or the desire sufficient, he may kill. Whether he plans the method or deliberates upon the act can make no difference. He is prompted by the instinct, and the reflection simply means the consideration of reasons for and against, or the reaching of inhibitions. If he acts, it is one of the primal emotions that causes the act. He is the "machine" through which certain emotions find their path and do their work. Infinite are the causes and circumstances that give rise to an emotion strong enough to take human life.

Killings which result from a sudden passion are easily understood. Everyone has been overwhelmed by rage, where reason and judgment and all acquired restraints are entirely submerged. The primitive man with his primitive emotion reasserts himself. It is mainly accident or the lack of some particular circumstance that prevents a murder. Of course some people are overwhelmed more easily than others. Some natures are less stable, some nervous systems less perfect, and the built up barriers are weaker. The whole result of stimuli is determined by the strength of the feeling acting upon the machine. Such a person is not ordinarily dangerous to the community. The act itself would generally assure that it could never happen again. Some killings, however, are more deliberate.

They are preceded by a settled hatred which preys upon the mind and fights against the preventive influences that training and habit have formed. Under a certain combination of circumstances these restrictions are swept aside and the emotions have their way.

There are, of course, certain broad classifications of homicides. A considerable number, perhaps more than any other, come through the commission of robbery, burglary and larceny. In the midst of the act the offender is caught, and kills in an effort to escape. These murders fall under the heading of property crimes; the cause is the same, and the rules governing them are the same. The second group, with respect to numbers, grows from the relations of men and women. Wives kill husbands and husbands kill wives; sweethearts kill each other. Jealousy and revenge are commonly mixed with sex life and sex association. Many socialists have argued that under an equal distribution of property, where women were freed from fear of want, these crimes would disappear. But this argument does not take human nature into account. Jealousy is inevitably associated with sex relations. The close contact of men and women over long periods of time inevitably causes friction and misunderstanding. These conditions often grow chronic, and in marriage are aggravated by the necessity of close association regardless of the real feelings that may exist. Certain claims are made by husbands and by wives, which are probably inherent in the relationship; sometimes they flow from habit and custom, but, from whatever cause, such claims are so exacting that either the husband or wife finds them hard to meet.

Because of the fact that the feelings of men and women for each other are deeper and more fundamental than those of any other relation, they are more subject to misfortune and tragedy. The hatreds born from the deepest affection are most beyond control. Then the desire of possession is overwhelming. It would be strange if more killings did not result from the relations of men and women than from any other cause. It is easy to understand why this is true. It is likewise easy to understand how laws, reason and judgment are powerless to prevent. Juries seem to understand this when women kill husbands and lovers, but a long-established code of chivalry and a cultivated attitude toward women, which is partly right and partly wrong, make it impossible to see that men are just as helpless under strong feelings as women. No doubt a public opinion that would favor divorces on a greater number of grounds and make them easily obtainable would prevent large numbers of such killings, but the cause can not be altogether removed.

The law has long singled out killing as the

greatest crime, doubtless because man prizes life first of all. Of course every effort should be made to protect life. Still, in measuring the character of the offender, in determining his possibilities as a useful citizen, homicide is probably one of the lesser crimes. Many times it implies no moral turpitude, even with those who believe in moral turpitude. It may imply very little lack of physical stability. Homicide practically never becomes an occupation. Most killings are accidental in the sense that they are casual and dependent on circumstances, and there is as a rule much less danger of repetition than there is of the original commission of a homicide by one of a defective nervous system who has never before committed an unlawful act. A large number of men convicted of murder are used as "trusties" in our penal institutions, even when their imprisonment is for a long term, or for life. This shows from the experience of prison officials that this class of offenders is, as a rule, of a better fibre than almost any other class.

Doubtless no sort of treatment will ever entirely get rid of homicide. Brains and nervous systems are so made, that inhibitions are unable to protect in all cases. Nations and men readily engage in killing, either from sport or because of a real or fancied wrong. Mob psychology shows how whole communities are turned into ravenous beasts, hunting for their prey. The world war, and all wars, show cases of mob psychology that have led large masses of men to take an active part in killing. The pursuit of those charged with crime shows that all people like the chase when the emotions are thoroughly aroused. Under certain impulses, communities gloat over hangings and commend judges and juries because they have the courage to hang, when, in fact, they were too cowardly not to hang and when their reason did not approve the verdict and judgment. Men who do not kill often wish others might die and are pleased and happy when they do die. We approve of death when it is the right one who dies. Whether all persons are murderers or not may depend upon a definition of murder. But, beyond doubt, all persons are potential murderers, needing only time and circumstances, and a sufficiently overwhelming emotion that will triumph over the weak restraints that education and habit have built up, to control the powerful surging instincts and feelings that Nature has laid at the foundation of life.

XI

SEX CRIMES

Most of the inmates of prisons convicted of sex crimes are the poor and wretched and the plainly defective. Nature, in her determination to preserve the species, has planted sex hunger very deep in the constitution of man. The fact that it is necessary for the preservation of life, and that Nature is always eliminating those whose sex hunger is not strong enough to preserve the race, has overweighted man and perhaps all animal life with this hunger. At least it has endowed many men with instincts too powerful for the conventions and the laws that hedge him about.

Rape is almost always the crime of the poor, the hardworking, the uneducated and the abnormal. In the man of this type sex hunger is strong; he has little money, generally no family; he is poorly fed and clothed and possesses few if any attractions. He may be a sailor away from women and their society for months, or in some other remote occupation making his means of gratifying this hunger just as impossible. There is no opportunity for him except the one he adopts. It is a question of gratifying this deep and primal instinct as against the weakness of his mentality and the few barriers that a meagre education and picked-up habits can furnish; and when the instinct over-balances he is lost.

Incest, which is peculiarly the crime of the weak, the wretched and the poor, has a somewhat different origin. Westermarck in his "*History of Human Marriage*" shows that in the early tribe there was no inhibition against the marriage of blood relations; that the restriction then was against the members of the tribe that used one tent; these might or might not be blood relations. The traditions and folk-ways against the marriage of close relations grew from the familiarity that came from the living together of brother and sister, for instance, in one home. This feeling gradually worked itself into custom and habit and from that into folk-ways and laws. Sometimes we read accounts of the marriage of a man and woman who found, after years had gone by, that they were brother and sister who had been separated in infancy and grew up without knowledge of their relation to each other. Whether Nature forbids the marriage of relatives by preventing offspring or by producing imperfect offspring is a doubtful question. Certain communities in Europe have lived together so long that all are related and still they seem to thrive. Considering the general custom and feeling on the subject, however, the man and woman who know that they are closely related and who marry are different and weaker than the others; and this may show in their offspring. Although the subnormal may have no such feeling, they are judged by the traditions and customs of the normal and on that judgment are sent to prison.

Many sex crimes are charged to children in the adolescent age; children who have no knowledge of sex and its development and are helpless in the strength of their newly-discovered feelings. This class of offenders is almost always the inferior and the poor who are moved by strong instincts which they have not the natural feeling, the strength, the education, nor the desire to withstand.

While most crimes against persons are not directly due to economic causes, still the indirect effect of property is generally present in these crimes as well as others. The fact that the poor and defective are generally the subjects of prosecution and conviction in these offences shows how closely economic conditions are related to all crimes.

Other criminal statutes are of more modern date, and as a rule involve not much more than adultery, except in regard to the age of the girl offender, which is generally placed below eighteen. Still the sex age of neither boys nor girls can be fixed by a calendar. It depends really upon development, which is not the same with all people or in all environments. Many girls of sixteen are more mature and have more experience of life than others of twenty. Most laws provide that below sixteen one cannot give consent and that a sexual act is then rape. It is doubtful if there should be any intermediate age between sixteen and eighteen, where an act is not rape but still a minor offence.

XII

ROBBERY AND BURGLARY

Robbery and burglary are generally counted as crimes of violence, but they should be properly classed under property crimes. Every motive that leads to getting property in illegal ways applies to these crimes. There is added to the regular causes of property crimes the element of danger and adventure which makes a strong appeal to boys and men. I am inclined to think that few mature men have committed one of these crimes, unless they began criminal careers as boys. Such crimes especially appeal to the activity and love of adventure which inhere in every boy. They are committed for the most part by youths who have had almost no chance to get the needed sport and physical experience incident to boyhood. The foot-ball, base-ball, polo or golf player very seldom becomes a robber or a burglar. Almost no rich man or rich man's son becomes a robber or a burglar. Those who fall under this lure are mainly the denizens of the streets, the railroad yards, the vacant lots, the casual workers who are stimulated by a variety of conditions to get property unlawfully. Added to this are almost invariably a defective heredity, vicious environment, little education, and a total want of direction in the building up of habits and inhibitions.

The robber or burglar who kills in the commission of crime is more dangerous and harder to cure than the one who kills from passion or malice. There is always the element of an occupation, for getting property, and generally a love of adventure that is difficult to overcome, except by a substantial change of social relations which makes acquiring property easier for the class from which all these criminals develop. The murder that comes from passion and feeling implies situations and circumstances that are rarely strong enough to overcome the restrictions against killing.

XIII

MAN AS A PREDATORY ANIMAL

Not less than eighty per cent of all crimes are property crimes, and it seems probable that, of the rest, most arise from the same motives. If we look at civilization as the result of that see-saw trend of the race from " Naturalism to Artificialism," we may get a flexible view of life that will be in accordance with the facts, and will help us to get rid of the arbitrary division of man's history into the three periods termed Savagery, Barbarism and Civilization. However desirable this division may be for historic purposes in general, it is only confusing in an effort to study the nature of man.

In the life and origin of the race, the fact is always evidenced that the Ego through its growth and persistence is always drawing to itself from the current of environment all things which it feels desirable to its life and growth. This must be a necessary condition of survival. In the long journey from amœba to man, any circumstance causing a complete halt for even a brief period meant extinction, while even a persistent interference produced a weakened organism, if not an arrest of development.

This then is the origin of the "Master Instinct," hunger. When we consider the various emotions growing from the force of this vital urge, as developed by adaptation to an ever-changing environment, we are able to realize fully why it bulks so large in moulding and shaping the destiny of the race.

All psychologists are agreed in classing under the nutritive instinct such activities as acquisition, storing and hoarding. During a period variously estimated as a quarter of a million to two million years, man and his animal antecedents responded to the hunger instinct, in the manner and by the same methods as did the various jungle animals. He secured his prey by capture, or killed it wherever found, the one condition being his power to get and to hold. Later tribal organization arose, and food and shelter were held in common. But since the folk-ways commended raiding and looting between alien tribes, here was presented an alluring chance to secure both booty and glory to men trained in the "get and hold" process of acquiring. For thousands of years life itself depended upon this unerring exercise.

It was during the period outlined that man developed his big brain (cerebrum) involving the central nervous system. Furthermore, it was developed by, and trained to, these particular reactions. The far-reaching control of the mind must be remembered, as upon this through his racial heritage must be based his conflicting impulses. These must be reckoned with in our conclusions with regard to present-day behavior, economic or otherwise.

During the last thirty years, psychological laboratories, aided by physiology, through oft-repeated experiments conducted with newly-invented weighing and measuring instruments of marvelous accuracy, have put us in possession of an array of facts unknown to students of earlier periods, who sought the "why and the how" of man's erratic actions as a social animal. It is constantly being demonstrated that under given conditions, moved by appropriate stimuli, the human animal inevitably and surely reacts the same as does inorganic matter. If we understand "intelligence" to be the "capacity to respond to new conditions," we can measurably see and at least partly understand the constant inter-play of heredity and environment. Between these there is no antagonism. The sum of life experiences consists solely in the adjustments required to enable the sentient organism — man or beast — to live.

How readily a "throw-back" to earlier and cruder life may be brought about under favorable conditions, is shown by the methods and virulence of combat during the vicious massacre in the war just ended. Can the conclusion be evaded that individually and collectively we constantly teeter on the brink of a precipice? If we fall it spells crime or misfortune, or both.

Wherever civilization exists on the private property basis as its main bulwark, we find crime as an inseparable result. Man, by virtue of his organic nature, is a predatory animal. This does not mean that he is a vicious animal. It simply means that man, in common with the eagle and the wolf, acts in accordance with the all-impelling urge and fundamental instincts of his organic structure. In any conflict between newer and nobler sentiments and the emotions which function through the primeval instincts, he is shackled to the bed-rock master instincts in such manner that they usually win. This is conclusively shown by the history of the race.

If this is true, we should expect to find the master hunger specially active through the many chances presented for exploitation after the fall of feudalism — beginning, let us assume, with the invention of power machinery — the "Age of Steam". It is apparent that from that time to our own day, man's acquisitive tendency has so expanded, that if we were capable of an unbiased opinion it might be said to be a form of megalomania gripping the entire white race, where highly-developed commerce and industry are found in their most vigorous forms.

If our theory is correct, we should expect to find the most energetic and enterprising nations showing a greater ratio of property crimes than the invalid and feeble nations. This would more certainly be true where political constitutions by letter and spirit encourage and promote individual development, mental and industrial. When this condition exists with abundant natural resources, such as often may be found in what we term a new country, it furnishes the chance for the most vigorous functioning of whatsoever may be the dominant qualities inherent in the tendencies and aspirations of a people. The United States of America, among the nations, meets these conditions, and we find here the highest ratio of property crimes per capita. This holds as to all such crimes, both minor and major, which are far in excess of those of any other nation, as shown by statistics.

It seems clear that this explanation shows the main reason for the seemingly abnormal number of property crimes in the United States.

Man's infinitely long past developed the hunger instinct, which made him take directly and simply where he could and as he could. This is always urging him to supply his wants in the simplest way, regardless of the later restrictions that modern civilization has placed around the getting of property. With the weaker intellectually and physically, these instincts are all-controlling. The superficial and absurd theories that his excesses are due to the lack of the certainty of punishment take no account of the life experience, and the inherent structure of man.

Especially in our large cities with their great opportunities for the creation and accumulation of wealth, the "lust of power" is shown by the nerve-racking efforts to obtain wealth by the most reckless methods. The emotion drives us to spend extravagantly and conspicuously, that we may inspire the envy of our neighbors by our money and power.

This is an old emotion securing a new outlet, and tenfold magnified in force, through modern conditions in commercial and industrial life. Is it not plain that in America it has assumed the form of an obsession, biting us high and low, until we reek of it? It is likewise clear that it is a menace to any abiding peace and welfare; that it is still growing and leaving a bitter harvest of neurasthenics in its wake.

The criminologist must face the fact that, in spite of contrary pretenses by most of our social doctors, we are still in our work-a-day life guided almost exclusively by the mores — the folk-ways of old — founded on expediency as revealed by experiences, and acquired by the only known process, that of trial and error. If this be true, it clearly follows that in order to conserve any vestige of a civilization, we must realize the fact that property crimes are the normal results of the complex activities making up the treadmill called civilization. We must likewise realize that to modify these crimes we must modify the trend of the race.

When the seamy side of man's behavior is scrutinized by science, it cannot be other than grim and distressing to the reader. It is this to the writer. But all the really significant facts of life are grim and often repulsive in the material presented. To the "irony of facts" must be ascribed the shadows as well as the high lights. No distortions or speculations can influence the findings of science. They are accessible and can be checked up by any one sufficiently interested. The student knows that man is what he is, because of his origin and long and painful past.

XIV

CRIMES AGAINST PROPERTY

By far the largest class of crimes may be called crimes against property. Strictly speaking, these are crimes in relation to the ownership of property; criminal ways of depriving the lawful owner of its possession.

Many writers claim that nearly all crime is caused by economic conditions, or in other words that poverty is practically the whole cause of crime. Endless statistics have been gathered on this subject which seem to show conclusively that property crimes are largely the result of the unequal distribution of wealth. But crime of any class cannot safely be ascribed to a single cause. Life is too complex, heredity is too variant and imperfect, too many separate things contribute to human behavior, to make it possible to trace all actions to a single cause. No one familiar with courts and prisons can fail to observe the close relation between poverty and crime. All lawyers know that the practice of criminal law is a poor business. Most lawyers of ability refuse such practice because it offers no financial rewards. Nearly all the inmates of penal institutions are without money. This is true of almost all men who are placed on trial. Broad generalizations have been made from statistics gathered for at least seventy-five years. It has been noted in every civilized country that the number of property crimes materially increases in the cold months and diminishes in the spring, summer and early autumn. The obvious cause is that employment is less regular in the winter time, expenses of living are higher, idle workers are more numerous, wages are lower, and, in short, it is harder for the poor to live. Most men and women spend their whole lives close to the line of want; they have little or nothing laid by. Sickness, hard luck, or lack of work makes them penniless and desperate. This drives many over the uncertain line between lawful and unlawful conduct and they land in jail. There are more crimes committed in hard times than in good times. When wages are comparatively high and work is steady fewer men enter the extra-hazardous occupation of crime. Strikes, lockouts, panics and the like always leave their list of unfortunates in the prisons. Every lawyer engaged in criminal practice has noticed the large numbers of prosecutions and convictions for all sorts of offences that follow in the wake of strikes and lockouts.

The cost of living has also had a direct effect on crime. Long ago, Buckle, in his "*History of*

Civilization," collected statictics showing that crime rose and fell in direct ratio to the price of food. The life, health and conduct of animals are directly dependent upon the food supply. When the pasture is poor cattle jump the fences. When food is scarce in the mountains and woods the deer come down to the farms and villages. And the same general laws that affect all other animal life affect men. When men are in want, or even when their standard of living is falling, they will take means to get food or its equivalent that they would not think of adopting except from need. This is doubly true when a family is dependent for its daily bread upon its own efforts.

Always bearing in mind that most criminals are men whose equipment and surroundings have made it difficult for them to make the adjustments to environment necessary for success in life, we may easily see how any increase of difficulties will lead to crime. Most men are not well prepared for life. Even in the daily matter of the way to spend their money, they lack the judgment necessary to get the most from what they have. As families increase, debts increase, until many a man finds himself in a net of difficulties with no way out but crime. Men whose necessities have led them to embezzlement and larceny turn up so regularly that they hardly attract attention. Neither does punishment seem to deter others from following the same path although the danger of detection, disgrace and prison is perfectly clear.

Sometimes, of course, men of education and apparent lack of physical defect commit property crimes. Bankers often take money on deposit after the bank is insolvent. Not infrequently they forge notes to cover losses and in various ways manipulate funds to prevent the discovery of insolvency. As a rule the condition of the bank is brought about by the use of funds for speculation, with the intention of repaying from what seems to be a safe venture. Sometimes it comes through bad loans and unforeseen conditions. Business men and bankers frequently shock their friends and the community by suicide, on disclosures showing they have embezzled money to use on some financial venture that came to a disastrous end.

These cases are not difficult to understand. The love of money is the controlling emotion of the age. Just as religion, war, learning, invention and discovery have been the moving passions of former ages, so now the accumulation of large fortunes is the main object that moves man. It does not follow that this phase will not pass away and give place to something more worth while, but while it lasts it will claim its victims, just as other strong emotions in turn have done. The fear of poverty, especially by those who have known something of the value of money, the desire for the power that money brings, the envy of others, the opportunities that seem easy, all these feelings are too strong for many fairly good "machines," and bring disaster when plans go wrong.

Only a small portion of those who have speculated with trust funds are ever prosecuted. Generally the speculation is successful or at least covered up. Many men prefer to take a chance of disgrace or punishment or death rather than remain poor. These are not necessarily dishonest or bad. They may be more venturesome, or more unfortunate; at any rate, it is obvious that the passion for money, the chance to get it, the dread of poverty, the love of wealth and power were too strong for their equipment, otherwise the pressure would have been resisted. The same pressure on some other man would not have brought disaster.

The restrictions placed around the accumulation of property are multiplying faster than any other portions of the criminal code. It takes a long time for new customs or habits or restraints to become a part of the life and consciousness of man so that the mere suggestion of the act causes the reaction that doing it is wrong. No matter how long some statutes are on the books, and how severe the penalties, many men never believe that doing the forbidden act is really a crime. For instance, the violations of many revenue laws, game laws, prohibition laws, and many laws against various means of getting property are often considered as not really criminal. In fact, a large and probably growing class of men disputes the justice of creating many legal rules in reference to private property.

Primitive peoples, as a rule, held property in common. Their inhibitions were few and simple. They took what they needed and wanted in the easiest way. There is a strong call in all life to hark back to primitive feelings, customs and habits. Many new laws are especially painful and difficult to a large class of weak men who form the bulk of our criminal class.

To understand the constant urge to throw off the shackles of civilization, one need but think of the number of men who use liquor or drugs. One need only look at the professional and business man, who at every opportunity leaves civilization and goes to the woods to kill wild animals or to the lakes and streams to fish.

The call to live a simple life, free from the conventions, customs and rules, to kill for the sake of killing, to get to the woods and streams and away from brick buildings and stone walls, is strong in the constitution of almost every man. Probably the underlying cause of the world war was the need of man to relax from the hard and growing strain of the civilization that is continually weaving new fetters to bind him. There must always come a breaking point, for, after all, man is an animal and can live only from and by the primitive things.

Children have no idea of the rights of property. It takes long and patient teaching, even to the most intelligent, to make them feel that there is a point at which the taking of property is wrong. Nowhere in Nature can we see an analogy to our property rights. Plants and animals alike get their sustenance where and how they can. It is not meant here to discuss the question of how many of the restrictions that control the getting of property are wise and how many are foolish; it is only meant to give the facts as they affect life and conduct.

It is certainly true that the child learns very slowly and very imperfectly to distinguish the ways by which he may and may not get property. His nature always protests against it as he goes along. Only a few can ever learn it in anything like completeness. Many men cannot learn it, and if they learned the forbidden things they would have no feeling that to disobey was wrong. Even the most intelligent ones never know or feel the whole code, and in fact, lawyers are forever debating and judges doubting as to whether many ways of getting property are inside or outside the law. No doubt many of the methods that intelligent and respected men adopt for getting property have more inherent criminality than others that are directly forbidden by the law. It must always be remembered that all laws are naturally and inevitably evolved by the strongest force in a community, and in the last analysis made for the protection of the dominant class.

XV

ATTITUDE OF THE CRIMINAL

Probably the chief barrier to the commission of crime is the feeling of right and wrong connected with the doing or not doing of particular acts. All men have a more or less binding conscience. This is the result of long teaching and habit in matters of conduct. Most people are taught at home and in school that certain things are right and that others are wrong. This constant instruction builds up habits and rules of conduct, and it is mainly upon these that society depends for the behavior of its citizens. To most men conscience is the monitor, rather than law. It acts more automatically, and a shock to the conscience is far more effective than the knowledge that a law is broken. For the most part the promptings of conscience follow pretty closely the inhibitions of the criminal code, although they may or may not follow the spirit of the law. Each person has his own idea of the relative values attached to human actions. That is, no two machines respond exactly alike as to the relative importance of different things. No two ethical commands have the same importance to all people or to any two people. Often men do not hesitate to circumvent or violate one statute, when they could never be even tempted to violate another.

Ordinarily unless the response of conscience is quick and plain, men are not bothered by the infraction of the law except, perchance, by the fear of discovery. This is quite apart from the teaching that it is the duty of all men to obey all laws, a proposition so general that it has no effect. Even those who make the statement do not follow the precept, and the long list of penal laws that die from lack of enforcement instead of by repeal is too well known to warrant the belief that anyone pays serious attention to such a purely academic statement. No one believes in the enforcement of all laws or the duty to obey all laws, and no one, in fact, does obey them all. Those who proclaim the loudest the duty of obedience to all laws never obey, for example, the revenue laws. These are clear and explicit, and yet men take every means possible to have their property exempted from taxation — in other words, to defraud the State. This is done on the excuse that everyone else does it, and the man who makes a strict return according to law would pay the taxes of the shirkers. While this is true, it simply shows that all men violate the law when the justification seems sufficient to them. The laws against blasphemy, against Sunday work and Sunday play, against buying and transporting intoxicating liquors and smuggling goods are freely violated. Many laws are so recent that they have not grown to be folk-ways or fixed new habits, and their violation brings no moral shock. In spite of the professions often made, most men have a poor opinion of congressmen and legislators, and feel that their own conscience is a much higher guide for them than the law.

Religions have always taught obedience to God or to what takes His place. Religious commands and feelings, are higher and more binding on man than human law. The captains of industry are forever belittling and criticising all those laws made by legislatures and courts which interfere with the unrestricted use of property. None of this sort of legislation has their approval and the courts are regarded as meddlesome when they enforce it. The anti-trust laws, the anti-pooling laws, factory legislation of all kinds, anything in short that interferes with the unrestricted use of property by its owner are roundly condemned and violated by evasion. On the other hand, so much has been written and said in reference to the creation of the fundamental rights to own property, and these rights depend so absolutely upon social arrangements and work out such manifest injustice and inequality, that there is always a deep-seated feeling of protest against many of our so-called property laws. From those who advocate a new distribution of wealth and condemn the injustice of present property rights, the step is quite short to those who feel the injustice and put their ideas in force by taking property when and where they are able to get it.

For instance, a miner may believe that the corporation for which he works really has no right to the gold down in the mine. As he is digging he strikes a particularly rich pocket of high-grade ore. He feels that he does no wrong if he appropriates the ore. Elaborate means are taken to prevent this, even compelling the absolute stripping of the workman, and a complete change of clothes on going in and coming out of the mine.

Many laws are put on the books which are of a purely sumptuary nature; these attempt to control what one shall do in his own personal affairs. Such laws are brought about by organizations with a "purpose." The members are anxious to make everyone else conform to their ideas and habits. Such laws as Sunday laws, liquor laws and the like are examples. Then, too, every state or nation carries a large list of laws that men have so long violated and ignored, that they virtually are dead. To violate these brings no feeling of wrong, but only serves to make men doubt the evil of violating any law.

It is never easy to get a Legislature to repeal a law. Generally some organization or committee of people is interested in keeping it alive, and the members of the Legislature fear losing their votes. Social ideas are always changing. No laws or customs are eternal. The ordinary man, and especially the man under the normal, cannot keep up with all the shifting of a changing world. There is always a fraction of a community agitating for something new and gradually forcing the Legislature to put it into law, even against the will of the majority and against the sentiment of a large class of the community. The organization that wants something done is always aggressive. The man who wants to prevent it from being done is seldom unduly active or even alarmed. Many organizations are eager to get statutes on the books. One seldom hears of a society or club that is active in getting laws repealed. The constant change of law, the constant fixing of new values in place of old ones, is necessary to social life. This means putting new wine into old bottles, and wine that is much too strong for the bottles. Everybody can see why some particular law might be violated without a sense of guilt, but they cannot see how a law they believe in can be violated without serious obliquity.

Apart from this, there have always been crimes that were not of the class that implied moral wrong.

The acts of the revolutionist who saw, or thought he saw, visions of something better; the man who is inspired by the love of his fellow-man and who has no personal ends to gain; the man who in his devotion to an idea or a person risks his life or liberty or property or reputation, has never been classed with those who violate the law for selfish ends. The line of revolutionists, from the beginning of organized government down to the birth of the United States and even to the present time, furnishes ample proof of this. And still the unsuccessful revolutionist meets with the severest penalties. To him failure generally means death. Men who are fired with zeal for all new causes are forever running foul of the law. Social organization, like biological organization, is conservative. All things that live are imbued with the will to live and they take all means in their power to go on living. The philosopher can neither quarrel with the idealist who makes the sacrifice nor the organization that preserves itself while it can; he only recognizes what is true.

Men have always been obliged to fight to preserve liberty. Constitutions and laws do not safeguard liberty. It can be preserved only by a tolerant people, and this means eternal conflict. Emerson said that the good citizen must not be over-obedient to law. Freedom is always trampled on in times of stress. The United States suffered serious encroachments on liberty during the Civil War. During the last war, these encroachments were greater than any American could have possibly dreamed; and so far there seems little immediate chance for change. Still the philosopher does not complain. He sees human passion for what it is, a great emotion that holds men in its grasp, a feeling that nothing can stand against. Opposition is destroyed by force, and often blind, cruel, unreasoning force. Sometimes even worse, this force is created for selfish ends. There are always those who will use the strongest and highest emotions of men to serve their private, sordid ends. Changing social systems, new political ideas, the labor cause, all movements for religious, social or political change have their zealots; they are met by the force of convention and conservatism ready to defend itself, and the clash is inevitable. It is easy to distinguish this sort of action from the things done by those who are known as criminals. Their acts are done to serve personal ends. Society may always punish both, but all men of right ideas will understand that the motive is different, the equipment and capacity of the men are different, and they are only in the same class because they each violate the law and are each responsive to emotions and to feelings that are of sufficient strength to compel action.

XVI

THE LAW AND THE CRIMINAL

If one were ill with a specific disease and he were sent to a hospital, every person who touched him, from the time his disease was known until he was discharged, would use all possible effort to bring him back to health. Physiology and psychology alike would be used to effect a cure. Not only would he be given surroundings for regaining health and ample physical treatment, but he would be helped by appeals in the way of praise and encouragement, even to the extent of downright falsehood about his condition, to aid in his recovery.

If such is done of "disease," why not of "crime"? Not only is it clear that crime is a disease whose root is in heredity and environment, but it is clear that with most men, at least when young, by improving environment or adding to knowledge and experience, it is curable. Still with the unfortunate accused of crimes or misdemeanors, from the moment the attention of the officers is drawn to him until his final destruction, everything is done to prevent his recovery and to aggravate and make fatal his disease.

The young boy of the congested districts, who tries to indulge his normal impulses for play, is driven from every vacant lot; he is forbidden normal activity by the police; he has no place of his own; he grows to regard all officers as his enemies instead of his friends; he is taken into court, where the most well-meaning judge lectures him about his duties to his parents and threatens him with the dire evils that the future holds in store for him, unless he reforms. If he is released, nothing is done by society to give him a better environment where he can succeed. He is turned out with his old comrades and into his old life, and is then supposed by strength of will to overcome these surroundings, a thing which can be done by no person, however strong he may be.

For the graver things, the boy or man is taken to the police station. There he is photographed and his name and family record taken down even before he has had a hearing or a trial. He is handled by officers who may do the best they can, but who by training and experience and for lack of time and facilities are not fitted for their important positions. I say this in spite of the fact that my experience has taught me that policemen, as a rule, are kindly and human. From the police station the offender is lodged in jail. Here is huddled together a great mass of human wreckage, a large part of it being the product of imperfect heredities acted upon by impossible environments. However short the time he stays, and however wide his experience, the first offender learns things he never knew before, and takes another degree in the life that an evil destiny has prepared for him. In the jail he is fed much like the animals in the zoo. In many prisons the jailer is making what money he can by the amount he can save on each prisoner he feeds above the rate the law allows of twenty-five or fifty cents a day. In a short time the prisoner's misery and grief turn to bitterness and hate; hatred of jailer, of officers, of society, of existing things, of the fate that overshadows his life. There is only one thing that offers him opportunity and that is a life of crime. He is indicted and prosecuted. The prosecuting attorney is equipped with money and provided with ample detectives and assistants to make it impossible for the prisoner to escape. Everyone believes him guilty from the time of his arrest. The black marks of his life have been recorded at schools, in police stations and examining courts. The good marks are not there and would not be competent evidence if they were. Theoretically the State's Attorney is as much bound to protect him as to prosecute him, but the State's Attorney has the psychology that leads to a belief of guilt, and when he forms that belief his duty follows, which is to land the victim in prison. It is not only his duty to land him in jail, but the office of the State's Attorney is usually a stepping-stone to something else, and he must make a record and be talked about. The public is interested only in sending bad folks to jail.

No doubt there are very few State's Attorneys who would knowingly prosecute unless they believed a man guilty of the offense, but it is easy for a State's Attorney to believe in guilt. Every man's daily life is largely made up of acts from which a presumption of either guilt or innocence can be inferred, depending upon the attitude of the one who draws the inference.

To a State's Attorney or his assistants the case is one that he should win. All cases should be won. Even though he means to be fair, his psychology is to win. No lawyer interested in a result can be fair. The lawyer is an advocate trying to show that his side is right and trying to win the case. The fact that he represents the State makes no difference in his psychology. In fact, he always tells the jury that he represents the State and is as much interested in protecting the defendant as in protecting society. He does this so that the jury will give his statements more weight than the statements of the lawyer for the defense, and this very remark gives him an advantage that is neither fair nor right.

The man on trial is almost always poor. It is only rarely that a poor man can get a competent lawyer to take his case. He is often handed over to the court for the appointment of a lawyer. The lawyer has no time or money to prepare a defense. As a rule he is a beginner not fitted for his job. If he wishes to take the case, he wants it only for the experience and advertising that it will bring. He is handed a case to experiment on, just as a medical student is handed a cadaver to dissect. If the defendant is in jail, he has little chance to prepare his case. If the defendant had any money he would not know what to do with it. He is often a mentally defective person. His friends are of the same class and can do little to help him. The jury are told that they must presume him innocent, but the accusation alone carries with it the presumption of guilt, which extends to everyone connected with the case, even to the lawyer appointed to defend him. It is almost a miracle if the defendant is not convicted.

Perhaps he is taken out to be hanged—the last act that society can do for him, or the convicted man is sent to prison for a long or shorter term. His head is shaved and he is placed in prison garb; he is carefully measured and photographed in his prison clothes, so that if he should ever get back to the world he will forever be under suspicion. Even a change of name cannot help him. While in prison he works and lives under lock and key, like a wild animal, eager to escape. On certain days he is allowed to sit at a long table with other unfortunates like himself, and visit for an hour with mother or father or wife or son or daughter or friend on the other side. Other prisoners, so far as he can associate with them, are as helpless and hopeless and rebellious as he. How they will get out, and when, are their chief concerns. Many of their guards are very humane. Probably no one seeks to torture him, but the system and the psychology are fatal. He sees almost no one who approaches him with friendship and trust and a desire to help, except his family, his closest friends and his companions in misery. He knows that the length of his term is entirely dependent upon officials whom he cannot see or make understand his case. He snatches at the slightest ray of hope. He is in despair from the beginning to the end. No prison has the trained men who, with intelligence and sympathy, should know and watch and help him in his plight. No state would spend the money necessary to employ enough attendants and aids with the learning and skill necessary to build him up. Money is freely spent on the prosecution from the beginning to the end, but no effort is made to help or save. The motto of the state is: "Millions for offense, but not one cent for reclamation."

As all things end, prison sentences are generally finished. The prisoner is given a new suit of clothes that betrays its origin and will be useless after the first rain, ten dollars in cash, and he goes out. His heredity and his hard environment have put him in. Now the state is done with him; he is free. But there is only one place to go. Like any other released animal, he takes the same heredity back to the old environment. What else can he do? His old companions are the only ones who will give him social intercourse, which he needs first of all, and the only ones who understand him. They are the only ones who will be glad to see him and help him get a job. There is only one profession for which he is better fitted after he comes out than he was before he went in, and that is a life of crime. Of course, he is a marked man and a watched man with the police. When a crime is committed and the offender is not found, the ex-convict is rounded up with others of his class to see, perchance, if he is not the offender that is wanted. He is taken to the lock-up and shown with others to the witnesses for identification. Before this, the witness may have been shown his photograph in convict clothes. Perhaps they identify him, perhaps they do not; if identified, he may be the man or he may not be. Anyhow, he has been in prison and this is against him. Whenever he comes out and wherever he goes, his record follows him as closely as his shadow. Even his friends suspect him. They suspect him even when they help him.

Such is the daily life of these unfortunates. What can be done? I can see nothing that the officers of the law can do. Officers represent the people. They reflect mob psychology. Even though an officer here and there rises above the crowd, as he sometimes does, it is of no avail. His place soon is filled by someone else. If only the public would understand! If only the public were more intelligent, which in this case at least would mean more human! If only the statement I repeat so often could be understood! There are no accidents; everything is the result of law. All phenomena are a succession of causes and effects. The criminal is the result of all that went before him and all that surrounds him. Like every other mortal, he is a subject for pity and not for hatred. If society is not safe while he is at large, he must be confined and kept under guard and observation. He must be kept until he is safe and a favorable environment found for him. If he will never be safe for society, he should never be released. He must not be humiliated, made to suffer unduly, despised or harried. He must be helped if he can be helped. This should be the second, if not the first object of his confinement.

Assuming that the scientific attitude toward crime should be accepted by those who make public opinion, and that this should become crystallized into written law, the problem would be easy.

The officers of the state can, as a rule, be depended upon to deal properly and considerately with the known insane. The insane are more trying and difficult than the criminal. Courts and juries and the public, however, recognize their mental condition and do not visit them with vengeance. It is appreciated and understood that they cannot with safety be left at large; but they are given the care and consideration that their condition demands. If the criminal should be looked upon as are the creatures insane from natural causes, the State's Attorney could then be trusted to prepare the case and do the best he could for all concerned. The defendant would no longer be a defendant. His case would be under investigation; his past life would be shown, his credits as well as his debits; he would need no lawyer, not even a public defender; no jury would be required, and the uncertainties and doubts that hang around judgments would be removed. There would be little chance for a miscarriage of justice. Even should there be, it would result in the speedy release of one against whom the public bore no ill-will. One who was sick or insane would ordinarily not need a lawyer, as the state would bear him no malice and make no effort to do more than investigate the case and present the facts. The whole matter should be a purely scientific attempt to find out the best thing to be done both for the interest of the public and the interest of the man.

No doubt, in many cases, men are convicted who are perfectly innocent of the crime of which they are accused. This is especially true with the poor who can provide for no adequate defense and who perhaps have been convicted before of some misdemeanor or crime. This is also often true in cases where there is great prejudice against the defendant, either on account of the nature of the case or of the defendant on trial. For instance, during the recent war a wave of hysteria swept over the world, and courts and juries trampled on individual rights and freely violated the spirit of laws and constitutions. The close of the war left the same intense feelings of bitterness which made justice impossible in cases where the charge savored of treason, and involved criticism of the government, or advocacy of a change of political systems.

Questions of race, religion, politics, labor and the like have always awakened violent feelings on all sides, have made bitter partisans and strict lines of cleavage, and have made verdicts of juries and judgments of courts the result of fear and hatred. In spite of this, most of the inmates of prisons have done the acts charged in the indictments. Why they did them, their states of mind, the conditions and circumstances surrounding them, what can be done to make them stronger and better able to meet life are never ascertained, and few courts or juries have ever deemed these things proper subjects for consideration or in any way involved in the case.

In law every crime consists of two things: an act and an intent. Both are necessary to constitute legal guilt, and on the prevalent theory of moral guilt and punishment both are necessary to make up criminal conduct. There can be no legal or moral guilt unless one intends wickedness; unless he deliberately does the act because he wishes to do wrong and knows he does wrong. The question then of moral guilt, which is necessary to the commission of a criminal act, touches all the questions suggested and many more. Even if freedom of action is to some degree assumed, the question still remains as to the degree of guilt in fixing punishment and responsibility. The question involves the make-up of the man, his full heredity, so far as it can be known.

Most of every man's heredity is hidden in the mist and darkness of the past. He inherits more or less directly through an infinite number of ancestors, reaching back to primitive man and even to the animals from which he came. The remote ancestry is, of course, usually not so important as that immediately behind him. Still, plainly, his form and structure and the details of his whole machine, including the marvelously delicate mechanism of the brain and nervous system, are heritages of the very ancient past. Neither are the processes of inheritance well understood nor subject to much control. Often in the making of the man Nature resorts to some "throw-back" which reproduces the ancient heritage. This can be seen only in general resemblances and behavior, for the genealogical tree of any family is very short and very imperfectly known, and the poor have no past. In three or four generations at the most the backward trail is lost and his family merged with the species of which he forms but a humble part.

Enough, however, is known of ancestry and the infinite marks of inheritance on every structure as well as enough of the reaction of the human machine to the varied environment that surrounds it, to make it clear that if one were all-seeing and all-wise he could account in advance for every action of every man. More than this, he could see in the original, fertilized cell, all its powers, defects and potentialities and could, in the same manner, look down through the short years during which the human organism, grown from the cell, shall have life and movement, and could see its varied environment. If one could see this with infinite wisdom, he could infallibly tell in advance each step that the machine would take and infallibly predict the time and method of its dissolution. To be all-knowing is to be all-understanding, and this is infinitely better than to be all-forgiving.

To get this knowledge of the past of each machine is the duty and work of the tribunal that passes on the fate of a man. It can be done only imperfectly at best. The law furnishes no means of making these judgments. All it furnishes is a tribunal where the contending lawyers can fight, not for justice, but to win. It is little better than the old wager of battle where the parties hired fighters and the issue was settled with swords. Oftentimes the only question settled in court is the relative strength and cunning of the lawyers. The tribunal whose duty it is to fix the future place and status of its fellowmen should be wise, learned, scientific, patient and humane. It should take the time and make its own investigation, and it can be well done in no other way. When public opinion accepts the belief that punishment is only cruelty, that conduct is a result of causes, and that there is no such thing as moral guilt, investigations and sorting and placing of the unfortunate can be done fairly well. The mistakes will be very few and easily corrected when discovered. There will be no cruelty and suffering. The community will be protected and the individual saved.

Neither will this task be so great as it might seem at first glance. Trials would probably be much shorter than the endless, senseless bickering in courts, the long time wasted in selecting juries and the many irrelevant issues on which guilt or innocence are often determined, make necessary now. Most of the criminal cases would likewise be prevented if the state would undertake to improve the general social and economic condition of those who get the least. Only a fraction of the money spent in human destruction, in war and out, would give an education adapted to the individual, even to the most defective. It would make life easy by making the environment easy. Only a few of the defective, physically and mentally, would be left for courts to place in an environment where both they and society could live. Perhaps some time this work will be seriously taken up. Until then, we shall muddle along, fixing and changing and punishing and destroying; we will follow the old course of the ages, which has no purpose, method or end, and leaves only infinite suffering in its path.

XVII

REPEALING LAWS

It is comparatively easy to get a penal statute on the books. It is very hard to get it repealed. Men are lazy and cowardly; politicians look for votes; members of legislatures and Congress are not so much interested in finding out what should be done, as they are in finding out what the public thinks should be done. Often a law lingers on the books long after the people, no longer believing the forbidden thing to be wrong, have repealed it. The statute stays, to be used by mischievous people and by those who believe in the particular law.

Often the unthinking lay hold of a catch-word or a pet phrase and repeat and write it, as if it were the last word in social science and philosophy. General Grant, when president, stumbled on such a silly combination of words, and surface-thinkers have been repeating it ever since, simply because it sounds wise and pat. Grant once said that, "The way to repeal a bad law is to enforce it." Grant was not a statesman nor a philosopher. He was a soldier. He probably heard some one use this phrase, and it sounded good to him. Out of that has grown the further statement which courts and prosecutors have used to excuse themselves for the cruelty of enforcing a law that does violence to the feelings of the people. This statement is to the effect that so long as the law is on the books, it is the duty of officers to enforce it. The smallest investigation of the philosophy of law shows how silly and reactionary such statements are.

One thing should be remembered. Laws really come from the habits, customs and feelings of the people, as interpreted or understood by legislative bodies. When these habits and customs are old enough they become the folk-ways of the people. Legislatures and courts only write them down. When the folk-ways change the laws change, even though no legislature or judge has recorded their repeal.

Since Professor Sumner of Yale University wrote his important book, "*Folkways,*" there is no excuse for any student not knowing that this statement is true. As a matter of fact, no court ever enforced all the written laws, or ever would, or ever could. Only a part of the discarded criminal law is ever repealed by other laws. The rest dies from neglect and lack of use. It is like the rudimentary parts of the human anatomy. Man's body is filled with rudimentary muscles and nerves that, in the past, served a purpose. These were never removed by operations, but died from disuse. Every criminal code is filled with obsolete laws, some of them entirely dead, others in the course of dissolution. They cannot be repealed by statute so long as an active minority insists that they remain on the books. When the great mass no longer wants them, it is useless to take the trouble to repeal them. The fugitive slave law was never believed in and never obeyed, and it was openly violated and defied by the great mass of the people of the North. The Fourteenth and Fifteenth Amendments to the Federal Constitution, and the statutes passed to enforce them, providing political and civil equality for the black man, and forbidding discrimination on railroads, in hotels, restaurants, theatres and all public places, have never really been the law in any state in the Union. Their provisions have always been openly violated and no court would think of enforcing them, for the simple reason that public sentiment is against it. Laws condemning witchcraft and sorcery both in Europe and America did their deadly work and died, for the most part, without repeal. Sabbath laws of all sorts forbidding work and play and amusements are dead letters on the statute books of most states, in spite of many attempts to galvanize them into life. All kinds of revenue laws are openly violated. Most tax-payers of intelligence who own property violate the revenue law openly and notoriously, and all courts and officers as well as the public know it. Many laws which interfere with the habits, customs and beliefs of a large number of people, like the prohibition laws, never receive the assent of so large a percentage as to make people conscious of any wrong in violating them, and therefore people break them when they can. Often this class of laws is enforced upon offenders who believe the law is an unwarrantable interference with their rights, and thus causes convictions where no moral turpitude is felt.

Every new crusade against crime not only sweeps away a large amount of work that has been slowly and patiently done toward a right understanding of crime, but likewise puts new statutes on the books which would not be placed there if the public were sane. When it does not do this, it increases penalties which work evil in other directions and awe courts, juries, governors and pardon boards, not only preventing them from listening to the voice of humanity and justice, but causing them to deny substantial rights and wreak vengeance and cruelty upon the weak and helpless.

XVIII

IS CRIME INCREASING?

The question is often asked, Is crime increasing? Statistics of all kinds can be gathered on this subject. In the main they seem to show that crime is on the increase in most civilized countries. It is very unsafe to use statistics without at the same time considering all the questions on which conduct rests. An increase of crime, as shown by statistics, may mean that the records are kept more completely than in former times. It may mean temporary causes like bad times are adding to the number of arrests and convictions. It may mean new classifications. It may mean that figures are based on arrests instead of convictions. It may include misdemeanors with graver offenses. It may or may not include repeaters. Statistics in any field are useful, but usually for broad generalizations, and they must always be interpreted by men of experience who are not interested in the results. Still, on the whole, it is probable that statistics show that crime is on the increase. What have reason and human experience to say on the subject?

We should always bear in mind that crime can never mean anything except the violation of law, when the violator is convicted; that it has no necessary reference to the general moral condition of man. Is the number of criminal convictions growing, and if so why? In the first place, the criminal code is lengthening every year. When civilized man began making criminal codes, there were comparatively few things forbidden. The codes were largely made up of those acts which, in some form, have for ages been generally thought to be criminal. Religious beliefs, customs and habits were included in the penal statutes. So were such things as sorcery and witchcraft. Property was then not an important subject in man's activities. When the instinct to create and accumulate property began to rule life, the criminal code grew very rapidly. Complex business interests, combined with the constantly increasing value placed on property, were always calling for new statutes.

The same tendency, indirectly, demanded still other statutes until at the present time this class of crimes makes up a large part of the criminal code and is growing steadily each year. Then too, the necessity of property has called for the violation of this part of the criminal code more than any other, and it has naturally caused a considerable increase of crime. Man in his social and political activities is ever weaving and bending and twisting back and forth. For a number of years the universal tendency, especially in America, has been toward what is called "Social Control", the idea being that more and more people should be controlled in an increasing number of ways. Of course, if people are to be controlled they must be controlled by other people. This policy has been extended until we are ever pushing further into the regulation of the habits, customs and lives of all the individual members of the community. The majority, when it has the power, has never hesitated to force its ways of living, its ideas, customs and habits on the minority. The majority, when strong enough, has always assumed that it was right, and provided that others must live its way or not at all. The pendulum is now swinging far this way as is evidenced by prohibition, the persistent campaign for Sunday laws, and the growing belief in social control as a means of changing and directing humanity.

This has added to the criminal code and has increased the number of men in prisons. Two statutes of recent date in most of the states are responsible for a very large increase in the number of convicts. The conspiracy statute which is used today is a deliberate scheme on the part of prosecutors to get men into the penitentiary by charging an agreement or confederation of two or more persons to do something, which, if really committed, would be a misdemeanor, or no crime whatever. Under this charge, whether made specifically or in connection with another crime, the rules of evidence have been opened and relaxed until the wildest and most remote hearsay is freely admitted for the plain purpose of convicting men who have really been guilty of no specific act. It is in effect punishing one for his thoughts; the business of the court or jury being to find out whether in some particular he has an evil mind.

The statute forbidding the use of the "confidence game" in obtaining property sends to prison a constant stream of persons who, until a few years ago, would have been guilty of no crime. This law, as interpreted by the courts, really means the procuring of money by dishonest means. Under this statute the court and jury hear the evidence and say whether the means charged are dishonest or not. This, of course, leaves the law so that the temporarily prevailing power, perhaps only the prosecuting attorney, may send men to prison who take means of getting money that are not practiced or at least advocated by the ones who procure the passage and enforcement of the law.

Numberless ways used by the strong to get money are considered dishonest by a large class of men and women: exaggerated and lying advertisements, forestalling the markets, the acts and wiles of the professional salesman, misrepresenting goods and other methods that could never be catalogued because new ways are constantly coming to light. The logical end of all these indefinite and uncertain laws is to pass one statute providing that whoever does wrong shall be imprisoned, *et cetera, et cetera.* The law never can specify all the ways of doing wrong and many of the meanest and most annoying things have never been, and from the nature of things never can be, prohibited by the statutes. No man is a good citizen, a good neighbor, a good friend, or a good man just because he obeys the law. The intrinsic worth is determined mainly by the intrinsic make-up.

Civilization is all the while making it harder for men to keep out of prison. Especially do the weak and ignorant and poor find that environment is constantly creating more inhibitions as time goes on. While rules and customs are prohibiting more and more ways of getting property, the needs growing out of civilization are always increasing. The simple inexpensive life of the past has given place to a more complex way of living, which calls for greater expense and harder work. It has created rivalry and jealousy to get the things that others have, and has placed men in a mad race with each other which often leads to jail or death.

Students of biology are constantly noting the difficulty that hereditary human traits, which have been evolved for simple reactions and plain living, find in making the necessary adjustments to the extravagant demands and complicated environment of the present day. This departure from the old normal and simple environment, due largely to machinery and commerce, is not only destroying individual lives by the thousands, but is seriously threatening the whole social fabric.

The creation of new courts, like "Boys' Courts," "Juvenile Courts," "Courts of Domestic Relations," "Moral Courts," with their array of "Social Workers," "Parole Agents," "Watchers," *et cetera,* shows the growth of crime and likewise the hopelessness of present methods to deal effectively with a great social question. Numbers of people in our big cities are making their living from the abnormal lives of children. Whether they are doing good or not, or whether their service is unselfish, as much of it doubtless is, are both quite aside from the question. The important fact is that the present system brings no results and that the disease is growing.

Instead of any considerable number of people taking hold of the question of crime, as physicians have taken hold of disease, and seeking to find its cause and to remove that cause, we content ourselves with prosecuting and punishing and visiting with misery and shame, not only the boys and girls, the men and women, who are the victims of life, but the large number of fathers, mothers, brothers, sisters, sons and daughters, whose lives are ruined by a catastrophe with which at least they had nothing to do. If a doctor were called in to treat a case of typhoid fever, he would probably find out where the patient got his milk supply and his drinking water and would have the well cleaned out to stop the spread of typhoid fever through infection. A lawyer called to treat the same kind of a case, legally speaking, would give the patient thirty days in jail, thinking that this treatment would effect a cure. If at the end of ten days the patient were cured, he would nevertheless be kept in prison until his time was out. If at the end of thirty days the disease was more infectious than ever, the patient would be discharged and sent upon his way to spread contagion in his path.

The transgression of organized society in the treatment of crime would not be so great if students and scientists had not long since found the cause of crime. It would be hard to name a single man among all the men of Europe and America who have given their time and thought to the solution of this problem, who has not come to the conclusion that crime has a natural origin, and that the criminal for the most part is the victim of heredity and environment. These students have pointed the way for the treatment of the disease, and yet organized government that spends its millions on prosecutions, reformatories, jails, penitentiaries and the like, has scarcely raised its hand or spent a dollar to remove the cause of a disease that brings misery and despair to millions and threatens the destruction of all social organization! To the teaching of the student and the recommendations of the humane the mob answers back: "Give us more victims, bigger jails, stronger prisons, more scaffolds!"

Not only has the constant multiplication of penal laws helped without avail to fill jails, but the failure to repeal laws that are outgrown does its part. As already stated, there are many anti-social and annoying things that can be done without violating the law. This, no doubt, is responsible for some of the general statutes like that aimed at the confidence game that catches a victim when the crime is not clearly defined as in "robbery," "burglary," "larceny" and the like. Still it has been the general opinion of those who have studied crime and influenced the passage of penal laws, that criminal statutes should be clear and explicit so that all would know what they must not do. It is obvious that if one is to be punished simply for doing wrong, there could be no judges or juries or jailers condemning and punishing and no crowds shouting for vengeance. All do wrong and do it over and over again, and day by day. It is not only those specific things that the great majority think are wrong, but the graver offenses that are meant to be the subject of criminal codes. Of course, codes do not work out this way in practice. In effect, they forbid the things that the strongest forces of the community wish forbidden, things which may or may not be the gravest and most anti-social acts, but which at least seem to the strong to be most hostile to their interests and ruling emotions.

XIX

MEDICAL EXPERTS

So long as the ordinary ideal of punishment prevails, a crime must consist of an act coupled with an intent to do the thing, which probably means an intent to do evil. This is no doubt the right interpretation of intent, although cases can be found, generally of a minor grade, which hold that evil intent is not necessary to the crime. Under the law as generally laid down, insanity is a defense to crime when the insanity is so far advanced as to blot out and obliterate the sense of right and wrong or render the accused unable to choose the right and avoid the wrong. Of course, legal definitions of scientific terms, processes, or things, do not ordinarily show the highest wisdom. It is safe to say that few judges or lawyers have ever been students of insanity, of the relation of "will" to "conduct," or of other questions of science or philosophy. Each man confines himself to his field of operation, and the love of living does not induce him to go far from the matter in hand, which to him means the base of supplies.

The insane are exempted from punishment for crime on the ground that they are not able to prepare and attend to their cases when placed on trial and on the further ground that their "free will" is destroyed by disease or "something else," and therefore they could form no intent. In another place I have tried to point out the fact that the acts of the sane and the insane are moved by like causes, but this is not the theory of the law.

Insanity is often very insidious. Many cases are easily classified, but there is always the border line, the twilight zone, which is sure to exist in moral questions and in all questions of human conduct, and this is hard to settle. It is generally determined by the feelings of a jury, moved or not by the prejudice of the public, depending on whether the community has been lashed or persuaded to take a hand in the conduct of the case.

Lawyers and judges are not psychologists or pschiatrists, neither are juries. Therefore the doctor must be called in. As a rule, the lawyer has little respect for expert opinion. He has so often seen and heard all sorts of experts testify for the side that employs them and give very excellent reasons for their positive and contradictory opinions, that he is bound to regard them with doubt. In fact, while lawyers respect and admire many men who are expert witnesses, and while many such men are men of worth, still they know that the expert is like the lawyer: he takes the case of the side that employs him, and does the best he can. The expert is an every-day frequenter of the courts; he makes his living by testifying for contesting litigants. Of course scientific men do not need to be told that the receipt of or expectation of a fee is not conducive to arriving at scientific results. Every psychologist knows that, as a rule, men believe what they wish to believe and that the hope of reward is an excellent reason for wanting to believe. It is not my intention to belittle scientific knowledge or to criticise experts beyond such general statements as will apply to all men. I have often received the services of medical experts when valuable time was given without any financial reward, purely from a sense of justice. But all men are bound to be interested in arriving at the conclusion they wish to reach. Furthermore, the contending lawyers are willing to assist them in arriving at the conclusions that the lawyer wants.

It is almost inevitable that both sides will employ experts when they have the means. The poor defendant is hopelessly handicapped. He is, as a rule, unable to get a skillful lawyer or skillful experts. A doctor's opinion on insanity is none too good, especially in a case where he is called only for a casual examination and has not had the chance for long study. The doctor for the prosecution may find that the subject can play cards and talk connectedly on most things, and as he is casually visiting him for a purpose, he can see no difference between him and other men. This may well be the case and still have little to do with insanity. Experts called for the defense cannot always be sure that the patient truthfully answers the questions. A doctor must make up his mind from examining the patient, except so far as hypothetical questions may be used. In all larger cities, certain doctors are regularly employed by the prosecution. While it would be too much to say that they always find the patient sane, it is safe to say that they nearly always do. Especially is this true in times of public clamor, which affects all human conduct. A court trial with an insanity defense often comes down largely to the relative impression of the testimony of the experts who flatly contradict each other, leaving with intelligent men a doubt as to whether either one really meant to tell the truth. The jury knows that they are paid for their opinions and regards them more or less as it regards the lawyers in the case. It listens to them but does not rely upon their opinions. Expert testimony is always unsatisfactory in a contested case. Under present methods, it can never be any different.

There is another danger: juries do not know the difference in the standing, character and attainments of doctors, so the tendency is always to find the man who will make the best appearance and testify the most positively for his side. This is unfair to the expert, unfair to science, and unfair to the case.

The method for overcoming this difficulty that has received most sanction from students is that experts shall be chosen by the state and appear for neither side. This, like most other things, has advantages and disadvantages. State officials, or those chosen by the state, usually come to regard themselves as a part of the machinery of justice and to stand with the prosecuting attorney for conviction. It will most likely be the same with state defenders. No one who really would defend could be elected or could be appointed, and it would work out in really having two prosecutors, one nominally representing the defense. A defendant should be left to get any lawyer or any expert he wishes. No one can be sure that the state expert will be better than the others. All one can say is that state experts may not be partisans, but, in effect, this would mean that they would not be partisans for the defendant. The constant association with the prosecutor, the officers of the jail, the public officials, and those charged with enforcing the law, would almost surely place them on the side of the state. Such men must be elected or appointed by some tribunal. This brings them to the attention of the public and makes them dependent on the public. The expert's interest will then be the same as the interest of the prosecutor and the judge.

The prosecuting attorney is not a partisan. His office is judicial. He is not interested in convicting or paid for convicting, and yet, no sane person familiar with courts would think that the defendant could be safely left in his hands. Assuming he is honest, it makes little difference. Almost no prosecutor dares do anything the public does not demand. Neither, as a rule, has he training nor interest to study any subject but the law. The profounder and more important matters affecting life and conduct are a sealed book which he could not open if he would. Very soon under our political system the expert business would gravitate into the hands of politicians, the last group that should handle any scientific problem. I am free to confess the difficulties of the present system, but some other way may be even worse. It must always be remembered that this country is governed by public opinion, that public opinion is always crude, uninformed and heartless. In criminal cases there is no time to set it right. The position of the accused is hard enough at best. He is really presumed guilty before he starts. Every lawyer employed to any extent in criminal practice knows that in an important case his greatest danger is public opinion. He would not take the officers and attachés of the court as jurors, although they might be good men, for their interest and psychology would be always for conviction.

If defendants were not regarded as moral delinquents, if the examination implied no moral condemnation, if it was only a scientific investigation as to where to place him if he is anti-social, if public opinion supported this view, then experts should be appointed by the court. On this phase of the case there would be little need of experts. I would be willing to go further and say that then, too, the partisan lawyer, the hired advocate, should disappear. The machinery of justice would be all-sufficient to take care of the liberties of every man, to give him proper treatment in disease, to restore him to freedom when safe, and, when that time does come, the unseemly contest in courts will disappear, and justice, tempered with mercy, will have a chance.

XX

PUNISHMENT

Assuming that man is justified in fixing the moral worth of his fellow; that he is justified in punishment for the purpose of making the offender suffer; and that these punishments according to the degree of severity will in some way pay for or make good the criminal act or protect or help society or prevent crime or even help the offender or someone else, what finally is the correct basis of fixing penalties?

No science, experience, or philosophy and very little humanity has ever been considered in fixing punishments. The ordinary penalties are first: fines, which generally penalize someone else more than the victim; these with the poor mean depriving families and friends of sorely needed money, and the direct and indirect consequences are sometimes small and sometimes very great. These can be readily imagined. If instead of fines a prison sentence is given, a sort of decimal system has been worked out by chance or laziness or symmetry of figures; certainly it has been done wholly regardless of science, for there is no chance to apply science when it comes to degrading men and taking away a portion of their lives. Generally ten days is the shortest. From this the court goes to twenty, then thirty, then sixty, then three months, then six months, then one year.

Why not eleven days? Why not twenty-four days? Why not forty days? Why not seventy days? Why not four months or five, or eight or nine or ten months? Is there no place between six months in jail and a year in jail? The bids at an auction or the flipping of pennies are exact sciences compared with the relation between crime and punishment and the process of arriving at the right penalty. If in the wisdom of the members of the legislature the crime calls for imprisonment in the penitentiary, then the ordinary sentences run one, two, five, ten, fifteen, twenty, thirty years, and life, according to the hazard of the legislature, the whim of the court, the gamble of the jury, or the feeling and means of expression of the unthinking and pitiless crowd who awe courts and juries with their cries for vengeance.

Neither does punishment affect any two alike; the sensitive and proud may suffer more from a day in jail or even from conviction than another would suffer from a year. The various courts and juries of the different states fix different penalties. Even in the same state there is no sort of resemblance to the punishments generally given for similar crimes. Some jurisdictions, some juries and some courts will make these three or four times as severe as others for the same things. Some days the same judge will give a longer sentence than on other days. In this judges are like all of us. We have our days when we feel kindly and sympathetic toward all mankind. We have our days when we mistrust and dislike the world in general and many people in particular. Largely the weather influences those feelings. Therefore, the amount of time a person spends in prison may depend to a great extent on the condition of the weather at the time of conviction or when sentence is passed. The physical condition of judge or jury, and above all, their types of mind, are all-controlling. No two men have the same imagination: some are harsh and cruel; others kind and sympathetic; one can weigh wheat and corn and butter and sugar; one can measure water and molasses and gasoline. When one measures or weighs, one can speak with exactness regarding the thing involved. Justice and mercy and punishment cannot be measured or weighed; in fact there is even no starting point. The impossibility of it all makes many of the humane and wise doubt their right to pass judgment upon their fellow man. Society no doubt is bound by self-protection to resist certain acts and to restrain certain men, but it is in no way bound to pass moral judgments.

Under any system based on a scientific treatment of crime, men would be taken care of as long as it was necessary to restrain them. It would be done in the best possible way for their own welfare. If they ever were adjudged competent to enter society again, they would be released when that time came. Neither under a right understanding, and a humane, scientific and honest administration, would it be necessary that places of confinement should be places of either degradation or misery. In fact the inmate might well be put where he could enjoy life more than he did before he was confined. It might and should be the case also that he could produce enough to amply take care of himself and provide for those who would naturally look to him for support, and perhaps make compensation for the injury he had caused to someone else.

It is obvious that this cannot be done until men have a different point of view toward crime. In the last hundred years much has been done to make prisons better and to make more tolerable the life of the inmates. This has been accomplished by men who looked on criminals as being at least to a certain extent like other men.

Above all, as things are now, the prison inmate has no chance to learn to conform unless hope is constantly kept before him. He should be like the convalescing invalid, able from time to time to note his gradual progress in the ability to make the adjustments that are necessary to social beings. No patient in a hospital could be cured if he were constantly told that he could not get well and should not get well. His imagination should be enlarged by every means that science can bring to the teaching of man.

First of all there must be individual treatment. No one would think of putting hundreds or thousands of the ill or insane into a pen, giving them numbers, leaving them so that no capable person knows their names, their histories, their families, their possibilities, their strength or their weaknesses. Every intelligent person must know that this would inevitably lead to misery and death. The treatment of men in prison is a much more difficult problem than the care of the physically diseased. It requires a knowledge of biology, of psychology, of hygiene, of teaching and of life; it needs infinite patience and sympathy; it needs thorough acquaintance and constant attention. It is a harder task than the one that confronts the physician in the hospital, because the material is poorer, the make is more defective, and the process of cure or development much slower and not so easily seen.

No person is entirely without the sympathetic, idealistic and altruistic impulses, which after all are the mainsprings of social adaptation. Probably these innate feelings can be found in prisoners as generally as in other men. It is the lack of these qualities that often keeps men outside the jail. They " get by " where kindly and impulsive men fail. A large part of the crime, especially of the young, comes from the desire to do something for someone else and from the ease with which persons are led or yield to solicitation.

The criminal has always been met by coldness and hatred that have made him lose his finer feelings, have blunted his sensibilities, and have taught him to regard all others as his enemies and not his friends. The ideal society is one where the individuals move harmoniously in their various orbits without outside control. The governing power of a perfect order in its last analysis must be within the individual. A perfect system probably will never come. Men are too imperfect, too weak, too ignorant and too selfish to accomplish it. Still, if we wish to go toward perfection, there is no other road.

One of the favorite occupations of legislatures is changing punishments in obedience to the clamor of the public. In times of ordinary tranquility a penalty may even be modified or reduced, but let the newspapers awaken public opinion to crime by the judicious use of headlines and a hot campaign, let the members feel that there is a popular clamor and that votes may be won or lost, and the legislature responds. This is generally done without reference to the experience of the world, without regard to the nature of man, with no thought of the victim, and with no clear conception of how the legislation will really affect the public.

The demand is constantly made that such crimes as kidnapping, train robbing, rape and robbery should be punished with death, or at least with imprisonment for life. Irrespective of its effect on the criminal, what is the effect on the victim of the criminal? A man is held up on a lonely highway; the robber does not intend to kill. His face is exposed. If the penalty for robbery is life imprisonment, he kills to avoid detection. If it is death, he kills even before he robs. The same thing operates in rape, in burglary, and in other crimes. In all property crimes not only is no killing intended or wanted, but precautions are taken to guard against killing. All laws to make drastic penalties should really be entitled: "An Act to Promote Murder."

Making penalties too drastic destroys the effect meant to be produced. Public clamor does not last forever. Men grow tired of keeping their tongues wagging on the same subject all the time. A state of frenzy is abnormal and when it subsides the temperature not only goes back to normal, but as far below as it has been above. When the fury has spent itself jurors regain some of their human feeling and refuse to convict. History has proved this over and over again, and still politicians always seek to ride into power on the crest of the wave; when the wave moves back, they can easily go back with it. Even if the severe punishments should be continued without abatement, these soon lose their power to terrify. Communities grow accustomed to hangings; they get used to life sentences and long imprisonments and the severity no longer serves to awe. The cruelty serves only as a mark of the civilization of the day. Some day, perhaps, a wiser and more humane world will marvel at our cruelty and ignorance, as we now marvel at the barbarity of the past.

XXI

THE EFFECT OF PUNISHMENT ON OTHERS

The ordinary man who hears of a crime hates the criminal and wants him to suffer. He does not picture the malefactor as a man who, for some all-sufficient reason, has committed a dreadful act. Still less does he ask: "Has he a father or mother, a wife or children, brothers or sisters, and how are these affected by his deed?" No one can intelligently deal with the criminal without considering these. Practically no inmate of a prison stands alone. He is a member of a family or small social group, and inevitably the interests of these others are more or less closely bound up with his. If punishment is justified for its influence on society, these must be taken into account with the other members of the social organization.

The criminal, it must be remembered, is almost always poor. He has a mother, brothers and sisters, wife or children, dependent for support to a large extent, upon his casual earnings. He is placed in jail or the penitentiary and the family must make new adjustments to life. The mother or wife may go to work at hard labor for a small return; the children may be taken out of school and sent to stores or factories, be condemned to lives of drudgery that will often lead to crime. The family may be broken up and scattered through institutions and the poorest shelters. A complete transformation for the worse almost always comes over the home. It is safe to say that at least three or four are closely touched by the misfortune of every one. These lives must be readjusted, and the chances are that the new adjustments will not be equal to the old, if for nothing else than because the conviction is a serious handicap in their struggles. Let anyone go to a city jail on a visiting day and see the old mothers, the stunned and weeping wives, the little children, down to babes in arms, who crowd around the corridors to get a look at the man behind the bars. To them at least he is a human being with feelings and affections, with wants and needs. All of these can recount his many good qualities which the world cannot see or know. Their first step is to borrow or to sell what they can to provide means for his defense. Everything else is cast aside. Day after day they visit the jail and the lawyer, contriving means to save liberty or life. When the trial comes, they watch through its maze in a dazed, bewildered way. They know that the man they love is not the one who is painted in the court room, and at least to them he is not. If he is convicted and goes to prison for a term of years, then month by month the faithful family goes to see him for an hour in the prison, visiting across the table in open view of guards and others as unfortunate as they. The family follows all sorts of advice and directions and seeks out many hopeless clews for men of influence and position who can unlock prison doors. The weeks run into months and the months into years, and still many of them keep up their hopeless vigil; some are driven to drudgery, some to crime, some to destruction for the man whom the state has punished that society may be improved. It is safe to say that the state ruins at least one other life for every victim of the prison.

No provision is made for the dependent families of the wretched man. Ruthlessly society sends the man to prison and sees the daughter leave school, a mere child, and go to work. What becomes of her it does not know or care. It seems not to know that she exists. The state sees the convict's boy working at casual tasks and growing up on the streets, while his father is paying the penalty of his act. He may on this account follow his father to jail; it is not society's concern.

Assuming that an offender must be confined for the protection of society, as some no doubt must be, still the effect on the family and how to prevent its destruction should be among the first concerns in the disposition of the case.

XXII

EVOLUTION OF PUNISHMENT

Among primitive peoples the penal code was always short. Desire for property had not taken possession of their emotions. Their lives were simple, their adjustments few, and there was no call for an elaborate code of prohibited acts. Their punishments were generally simple, direct and severe: usually death or banishment which often meant death, sometimes maiming and branding, so that the offender might serve as a constant warning to others.

Primitive peoples early asked questions about their origin and destiny. The unknown filled most of the experiences of their lives. The realm of the known was very small. They had no idea of law and system, of cause and effect. They early began evolving religious ideas. The manifestations of nature, the mystery of birth, the fear of death, the phenomena of dreams, the growth and harvesting of crops — all of these were beyond their understanding. They peopled the earth with gods to be propitiated and appeased. Everything was the act of a special providence. From early times religion and witchcraft furnished the chief subjects for the criminal code.

The penalties for the violation of the code were always severe, generally death, and by the most terrorizing ways. No other crime could be so great as to arouse the anger of the gods, and naturally no other conduct should demand so severe a penalty as calling down the wrath of the gods. This would fall not only upon the offending man, but upon the community of which he was a part. Even as man developed in knowledge and civilization, this sort of crime continued to furnish the greater proportion of victims and the most cruel punishments. Torture of the most fiendish sort was evoked to catch offenders and extort confessions. Difference of religious opinions was the worst crime. The inquisition became an established thing. Sometimes a nation was almost wiped out that heretics should be killed and heresies destroyed. The heretic was the one who did not accept the prevailing faith. The list of victims of punishment on account of religion, witchcraft, sorcery and kindred laws has in the past no doubt been larger than for any other charges.

This kind of laws always called out the greatest zeal in their enforcement. To the religious enthusiast nothing else was of equal importance. It involved not only the life of man on earth but his life through all eternity. Our statutes today are replete with such crimes, but the punishments have been lessened and, as a rule, communities will not enforce them. But laws against blasphemy, working on Sunday, and Sunday amusements of all sorts, are still on the books and enforced in some places. A large organization and an influential and aggressive part of the Christian Church are insisting that these laws shall be enforced to the limit and that still others shall be placed among the statutes of the several states.

The methods of inflicting the death penalty have been various, the favorite ways being burning, boiling in oil, boiling in water, breaking on the rack, smothering, beheading, crucifying, stoning, strangling and electrocuting. Until the middle of the last century they were carried out in the presence of the multitude so that all might be warned by the example.

The number of crimes for which death and bodily torture have been the punishment can scarcely be recorded, and if they could it would be of no value. They would run into the hundreds and probably the thousands. A large part of these crimes are now obsolete. Doubtless more men have been executed for crimes they did not commit and could not commit than for any real wrong of which they were guilty.

Prisons came into fashion later than the death penalty, and as a form of punishment have gradually come to take the place of most death penalties. Prisons in the past have been loathsome places and not much better than death. Prisoners have been packed together so closely that life was almost impossible. To incarcerate victims in prisons has brought terrible punishment not only on the prisoners and their families, but indirectly on the state. No doubt through the years prisons have been gradually improved. Many of their terrors have been banished. People have come to believe that even a prisoner should have some consideration from the state. Penalties have likewise grown less severe and terms have been shortened, but this course has not been regular or constant; the public readily relaxes into hatred and vengeance, and it is easy to arouse these feelings in men, since they lie very close to the surface. A constant struggle has always been waged by the humane to make man more kindly, and yet probably his nature does not really change. A few months of frenzy may easily undo the work of years.

So long as men punish for the sake of punishment, there will be a disagreement between the advocates of long punishment and short punishment, hard punishment and light punishment. From the nature of things, there is no basis on which this can be determined. The only thing that throws any light on the question is experience, and men can always differ as to the lessons of experience. Neither do they remember experience when feelings are concerned.

Punishment can deter only on the ground of the fear that flows from it. Fear comes from things that are more or less unusual. Man has little abstract fear of a natural death; it is so unavoidable that it does not even figure in the ordinary affairs of life. Extreme punishments may grow so common that few give them any concern. They probably are so common now that the impression they make is not very great. Lighter and easier punishments would have the same psychological effect. In many cases a lenient punishment would also eliminate much of the hatred and bitterness against the world that are common to all inmates of prisons.

XXIII

CAPITAL PUNISHMENT

The question of capital punishment has been the subject of endless discussion and will probably never be settled so long as men believe in punishment. Some states have abolished and then reinstated it; some have enjoyed capital punishment for long periods of time and finally prohibited the use of it. The reasons why it cannot be settled are plain. There is first of all no agreement as to the objects of punishment. Next there is no way to determine the results of punishment. If the object is assumed it is a matter of conjecture as to what will be most likely to bring the result. If it could be shown that any form of punishment would bring the immediate result, it would be impossible to show its indirect result although indirect results are as certain as direct ones. Even if all of this could be clearly proven, the world would be no nearer the solution. Questions of this sort, or perhaps of any sort, are not settled by reason; they are settled by prejudices and sentiments or by emotion. When they are settled they do not stay settled, for the emotions change as new stimuli are applied to the machine.

A state may provide for life imprisonment in place of death. Some especially atrocious murder may occur and be fully exploited in the press. Public feeling will be fanned to a flame. Bitter hatred will be aroused against the murderer. It is perfectly obvious to the multitude that if other men had been hanged for murder, this victim would not have been killed. A legislature meets before the hatred has had time to cool and the law is changed. Again, a community may have capital punishment and nothing notable happens. Now and then hangings occur. Juries acquit because of the severity of the penalty. A feeling of shame or some bungling execution may arouse a community against it. A deep-seated doubt may arise as to the guilt of a man who has been put to death. The sentimental people triumph. The law is changed. Nothing has been found out; no question has been settled; science has made no contribution; the public has changed its mind, or, speaking more correctly, has had another emotion and passed another law.

In the main, the controversy over capital punishment has been one between emotional and unemotional people. Now and then the emotionalist is reinforced by some who have a religious conviction against capital punishment, based perhaps on the rather trite expression that "God gave life and only God should take it away." Such a statement is plausible but not capable of proof. In the main religious people believe in capital punishment. The advocates of capital punishment dispose of the question by saying that it is the "sentimentalist" or, rather, the "maudlin sentimentalist" who is against it. Sentimentalist really implies "maudlin."

But emotion too has its biological origin and is a subject of scientific definition. A really "sentimental" person, in the sense used, is one who has sympathy. This, in turn, comes from imagination which is probably the result of a sensitive nervous system, one that quickly and easily responds to stimuli. Those who have weak emotions do not respond so readily to impressions. Their assumption of superior wisdom has its basis only in a nervous system which is sluggish and phlegmatic to stimuli. Such impressions as each system makes are registered on the brain and become the material for recollection and comparison, which go to form opinion. The correctness of the mental processes depends upon the correctness of the senses that receive the impression, the nerves that transmit the correctness of the registration, and the character of the brain. It does not follow that the stoic has a better brain than the despised "sentimentalist." Either one of them may have a good one, and either one of them a poor one. Still, charity and kindliness probably come from the sensitive system which imagines itself in the place of the object that it pities. All pity is really pain engendered by the feelings that translate one into the place of another. Both hate and love are biologically necessary to life and its processes.

Many people urge that the penalty of imprisonment for life would be all right if the culprit could be kept in prison during life, but in the course of time he is pardoned. This to me is an excellent reason why his life should be saved. It is proof that the feeling of hatred that inspired judge and jury has spent itself and that they can look at the murderer as a man. Which decision is the more righteous, the one where hatred and fear affect the judgment and sentence, or the one where these emotions have spent their force?

Everyone who advocates capital punishment is really ashamed of the practice for which he is responsible. Instead of urging public executions, the most advanced and sensitive who believe in killing by the state are now advocating that even the newspapers should not publish the details and that the killing should be done in darkness and silence. In that event no one would be deterred by the cruelty of the state. That capital punishment is horrible and cruel is the reason for its existence. That men should be taught not to take life is the purpose of judicial killings. But the spectacle of the state taking life must tend to cheapen it. This must be evident to all who believe in suggestion.

Constant association and familiarity tend to lessen the shock of any act however revolting. If men regarded the murderer as one who acted from some all-sufficient cause and who was simply an instrument in an endless sequence of cause and effect, would anyone say he should be put to death?

It is not easy to estimate values correctly. It may be that life is not important. Nature seems extravagantly profligate in her giving and pitiless in her taking away. Yet death has something of the same shock today that was felt when men first gazed upon the dead with awe and wonder and terror. Constantly meeting it and seeing it and procuring it will doubtless make it more commonplace. To the seasoned soldier in the army it means less than it did before he became a soldier. Probably the undertaker thinks less of death than almost any other man. He is so accustomed to it that his mind must involuntarily turn from its horror to a contemplation of how much he makes out of the burial. If the civilized savages have their way and make hangings common, we shall probably recover from some of our instinctive fear of death and the extravagant value that we place on life. The social organism is like the individual organism: it can be so often shocked that it grows accustomed and weary and no longer manifests resistance or surprise.

So far as we can reason on questions of life and

death and the effect of stimuli upon human organisms, the circle is like this: Frequent executions dull the sensibilities toward the taking of life. This makes it easier for men to kill and increases murders, which in turn increase hangings, which in turn increase murders, and so on, around the vicious circle.

In the absence of any solid starting point on which an argument can be based; in the absence of any reliable figures; in the absence of any way to interpret the figures; in the absence of any way to ascertain the indirect results of judicial killings, even if the direct ones could be shown; in the impossibility through life, experience or philosophy of fixing relative values, the question must remain where it has always been, a conflict between the emotional and unemotional; the "sentimental" and the stolid; the imaginative and the unimaginative; the sympathetic and the unsympathetic. Personally, being inclined to a purely mechanistic view of life and to the belief that all conduct is the result of certain stimuli upon a human machine, I can only say that the stimuli of seeing and reading of capital punishment, applied to my machine, is revolting and horrible. Perhaps as the world improves, the sympathetic and imaginative nature will survive the stolid and selfish. At least one can well believe that this is the line of progress if there shall be progress, a matter still open to question and doubt.

XXIV

STIGMATA OF THE CRIMINAL

Lombroso and others have emphasized the theory that the criminal is a distinct physical type. This doctrine has been so positively asserted and with such a show of statistics and authority, that it has many advocates. More recent investigations seem to show conclusively that there is little or no foundation for the idea that the criminal is a separate type. Men accustomed to criminal courts and prisons cannot avoid being impressed with the marks of inferiority that are apparent in prisoners. Most prisoners are wretched and poorly nourished, wear poor clothes and are uncared-for and unkempt. Their stunted appearance is doubtless due largely to poor food, the irregularity of nourishment, and the sordidness of their lives in general. One also imagines that a prisoner looks the part, and in his clothes and surroundings he generally does. It is hard for a prisoner to look well-groomed; he has neither the opportunity nor the ambition to give much attention to his personal appearance. The looks of the prisoners are of little value. Nothing but actual measurements could give real information, and these do not sustain the theory of their being different from other men.

It is not possible to see how the criminal can be of a distinct physical type. Criminality exists only in reference to an environment. One cannot be born a criminal. One may be, and often is, born with such an imperfect equipment that he cannot make his adjustments to life, and soon falls a victim to crime and disease. All that a physical examination could do would be to show the strength or weakness of the body and its various organs. What may befall him will depend partly on the kind and quality of his mind and nervous system, and partly on the physical structure and the kind of experiences that life holds in store for him.

No doubt thorough psychological examinations would reveal something of the brain, just as physical examinations certainly would determine the strength and capacity of the body. This would be of material aid in determining the kind of environment that should be found for the individual, and if such environment could be easily found it would avert most of the calamities which beset the path of the youth.

Something can be told of a person's character from his eyes, the expression of the face and the contour of the head, but this information is very misleading as our everyday experience shows. It is not necessary to find stigmata in the prisoner to know that he was born the way he is., One's character must be fixed before birth whether Nature marks it on one's head or not. Likewise every particle of matter moves from stimuli and obedience to law, regardless of whether it shows in the face or not. The strong are no more exempt from the law than the weak. All the difference is that they can longer and more easily avoid disaster.

Everyone is in the habit of forming a hasty opinion of another by reading his face and noting his expression. But the indication given by facial expression is mainly the product of the life that has been lived, and tells something of the part that the hidden emotions have played on the body.

It has been generally believed that mind has its seat in the brain and the nervous system. Later investigations, however, seem to show that it is the product of the whole physical organism. There is no chance to measure or weigh or still less assay the qualities of the machine. It is certain that the quality of the mind depends very little upon either the contour or size of the skull.

About all that can be learned of the mind and the character of the man must be gathered from the manifestation of the machine. It is shown by his behavior in action and reaction. This behavior is caused by the capture, storage and release of energy through the ductless glands.

A defective mechanism either inherited or acquired through imperfectly balanced glands will inevitably produce an imperfect mind and defective conduct. This it will be bound to do because the body is the mind.

As a matter of fact, no man is branded physically with the " mark of Cain." If criminology were so simple it would not be difficult to handle. The manifestations of the human machine are infinite and only patience and careful study can find the points of weakness and of strength. That all brains and bodies have both is beyond dispute. No physical human structure was ever put together where the organs were equally strong to do the work assigned to them. Some part of the body always needs watchfulness and repair and can never be depended upon in emergencies. In times of overstress and strain, the defective organ or organs will manifest their weakness. The intricate nervous system and the brain, the unseen instincts and emotions likewise do not work perfectly; but as a rule the ones that underwork or overwork cannot be seen by a physical examination. It generally requires great subtlety to find them, and careful treatment and environment to make the machine work fairly well in spite of these imperfections. This could be provided; in most cases the machine could be placed in an environment where it would work fairly well; but instead of this all the effort that is made to keep the machine in shape is a threat of the jail if it goes wrong; it is then left to run itself without help or assistance of any kind.

While examinations of the head do not show marked differences between prisoners and others, a great distinction is seen between the general proportion and the degrees of nourishment of prisoners and those not accused of crime. Nothing is more common than the weak and underfed condition of the delinquent and the criminal. This needs no expert examination. It is obvious to all. The poor, scanty clothes and personal belongings corroborate the fact that the accused is poor and has not enough to eat or wear, nor anything but the most scanty shelter. In addition to these facts, he is almost always ill. A report recently published, based on investigations by a special committee of the New York State Commission of Prisons, shows that in the New York Reformatory only eight per cent passed the required physical examination. In the penitentiary, where the average age was higher, only five per cent passed the test. In the work house—the home of the "down and outs"—only one per cent passed. The health tests employed were those for admission to the army. It was likewise found by the same commission that of those in good health or fair physical condition, eighty-five per cent were self-supporting, while only eighteen per cent of those in poor physical condition took care of themselves.

Disease and ill health, when found so generally, are in themselves indications of a defective system, and such machines are constantly exposed to temptation. Their needs are ever present and their poverty great. Sickness and disease weaken or destroy such inhibitions as the unfortunate are able to build up, and they readily yield to crime.

XXV

THE GOOD IN CRIMINALS

The criminal is confronted in court with an indictment charging him with a violation of the law. He is a human being, like all others, neither perfect nor entirely worthless. He has some tendencies and inclinations which the world calls good for lack of a better term, and some that it calls bad for the same reason. In this he is like the jury and the judge. The strength of the different tendencies is not the same in any two machines. The judge and jury are interested in determining whether he is good or bad; that is, better or worse than they themselves. In theory he is tried on the charges contained in the indictment.

In most cases by a constant stretching of the rules of evidence his whole life may be involved. That is, proof may be offered of any act of delinquency that constituted a violation of the law, if in any way similar, or in any way connected with the one charged in the indictment. He cannot meet these charges by proving the acts of kindness and charity and real worth that are rarely absent in any life. The proceedings show how bad he is, not how good. He may be able to call witnesses to show that up to the time of the bringing of the indictment his reputation for honesty was good; but he cannot show that he supported his grandmother, or helped his aunt, or educated his younger brother, or gave his money to the poor. All the good is irrelevant to the issue. This does not prove that he did not commit the act. It might clearly prove whether on the whole he should go to jail. Through this process he feels that the law and proceedings are unfair and that he is condemned, when, in fact, he is as good as those who judge him. Neither can he show the circumstances that hedged in his way nor the equipment with which he entered life. Under the legal theory that he is "the captain of his soul," these are not material to the issue. Neither can he show the direct motive that caused the conduct. It may have been a motive that was ideal, but the question involved is, did he violate the law?

He is convicted and sent to prison. As a rule, he will some time be turned back into the world. He needs careful treatment, involving instruction and an appeal to that part of his nature which may awaken sympathies and produce emotions that will make him more of a social being on his return to the world. In the loose language of the world, it is necessary for him not only to learn how to curb the evil but how to increase the good. His imagination should be cultivated and enlarged. The responses to better sentiment should be strengthened. This can be furthered only by skilled teachers who are moved by the desire to help him. The process should be similar to a hospital treatment. Instead of this, he is usually surrounded by men of little intelligence or education, men who have no fitness for the task; he is governed by strict rules, all of them subjecting him to severe penalties when violated. Every action in the prison reminds him of his status. With the exception of a few strong men who need suffering for their development it can have but one result. He must come out from prison poorer material than when he went in. There are only two reflections that can keep him out of trouble in the future: the remembrance of the past and the fear that a similar experience might come to him again.

When it is remembered that the greatest enemy to happiness and life is fear; when we realize that the constant battle of the primitive man was with the fear that peoples the unknown with enemies and dangers; when we remember that in some way, fear of poverty, of disease, of disaster, of loss of friends and life is the ever-present enemy of us all, it is evident that nothing but harm can come from the lessons of fear that are drilled into the victim in prison. Life furnishes countless ways to be kind and helpful and social. It furnishes infinite ways to be cruel, hard and anti-social. Most of these anti-social ways are not condemned by the law. Whether the life is helpful and kindly or hard and selfish can never depend upon the response of an organism to fear, but upon the response of an organism to the kindlier and more humane and sympathetic sentiments that to some extent at least inhere in the constitution of man.

It is a common thing for prisoners, even during the longest term, to be more solicitous about mother, child, wife, brother or friend than about themselves. It is common for them to deny themselves privileges, presents or favors to help other inmates. The consideration and kindness shown by unfortunates to each other are surprising to those who have no experience with this class of men. Often to find real sympathy you must go to those who know what misery means. Pride and coldness are usually due to lack of understanding, and life alone can bring understanding. Every intelligent man engaged in efforts to improve and help either criminals or children or any others, knows the need of an appeal to what passes as the better nature. Help does not come so much from directly inhibiting the bad as by extending the area of the higher emotions. To pull up weeds in a garden without planting something in their place is a foolish task. The human being is like the garden. Something must grow in the soil. If weeds are pulled up and nothing planted Nature will grow more weeds. Some feelings and emotions always possess every person. The best that is incident to the machine should be found and this be cultivated and extended until it dominates the man. Courts and prisons have no machinery to cultivate the best in their victims; they are always looking for the worst, aiding and promoting it until the prisoner is driven to hopelessness and despair.

XXVI

THE DEFECTIVE AND INSANE

It is almost hopeless to bring any system or order out of the chaos that prevails in the discussion of the insane, the defective, the moron, and the feeble-minded. The world has so long believed that man is a specially created animal and that he does wrong from free choice, that much more time and investigation are necessary before sane and scientific theories can be formulated on this subject.

It has been a great many years since any semi-intelligent man believed that all sorts of physical abnormalities were due to one cause and could be cured by one method, and yet the prevailing opinion now, even among the fairly educated, is that all sorts of abnormal conduct are due to one cause, perversity and wickedness, and should be treated with only one prescription, punishment. Scientific men indeed have long known that there were causes for the abnormality of conduct and that there were various more or less satisfactory remedies for many cases. Still the time that scientists have worked on the problem is short and the data imperfect, and many years of patient study will be needed before there can be worked out the broad theories of responsibility for and treatment of crime which will replace the long accepted doctrines of original sin, and the expulsion of devils from the wicked by cruelty and punishment.

By far the largest part of the population of prisons is made up of the insane, feeble-minded, morons, defectives or victims of diseases that seriously influence conduct. This is especially shown by the increased percentage of the clearly defective that are repeaters, over those in prison for their first offense. There is no lack of statistics as to the various groups of defectives, but these figures cannot be reconciled. No two authorities agree as to percentages; the classifications are more or less uncertain; the dividing lines between the different groups are vague, one class easily fading into another. The investigations have largely been made by those not trained for the work, and above all the conclusions as to treatment are at variance, doubtful and necessarily not yet satisfactory. That the clearly insane and the plainly feeble-minded should not be punished would doubtless be admitted by all who speak in public or write for others to read. Many persons speaking in private, acting on juries and connected with the machinery of "justice" say that these should be punished like the rest. Still for a starting point, it may be assumed that most men would agree that these classes should be restrained rather than punished.

The chief difficulty is that between the most violently insane and the least emotional man are infinite numbers of gradations blending so closely that no one can mathematically or scientifically classify all the various individual units. While there are cases of insanity that can be clearly traced to injury or disease, the degree of sanity in most cases is still impossible to determine. Most insane people are sane on some things, generally on most things and are sane a part or most of the time. The periods of sanity and insanity can be distinguished only by conduct. How far any specific insanity may impair the brain and affect the inhibitions, is impossible to foretell.

When it comes to the defective, the problem is still more difficult. No two persons have the same degree of intelligence. Some are clearly lacking in mentality. Others are manifestly intelligent. The great mass range all along between these extremes. Various arbitrary rules have been laid down to aid in classifying different grades of defectives. Generally the feeble-minded can be sorted out. The defectives are supposed, if young, to be two years or more below the normal scholar in development; if older, three or more below. Their standing is fixed by asking certain test questions. Furthermore, a list of questions has been commonly used for an "intelligence test." These queries have nothing to do with the school work of the child, but are supposed to reveal only his native intelligence.

No doubt in a broad way such tests throw considerable light on the mentality of those who submit to the examination. Ordinary experience, however, shows that they cannot be fully relied on. Some children develop very slowly, others very rapidly. Some are much quicker, others slower in their perceptions and responses. No two children or grown-ups have the same turn of mind. One may be very bright in business affairs and very dull in books. One may be clever in arithmetic and hopeless in grammar. One may have marked mechanical ability and no taste for school. These tests are only valuable if given by well qualified examiners, and the method is so new that few have had the chance to thoroughly prepare for the work. For the most part the tests are given by people who are wholly unfit for so important a task.

Quite aside from all this it is not certain that intelligent people are necessarily safer to the community than stupid ones. There is always a tendency for the stupid to stick to the beaten path. Intelligence generally means individuality and divergence. On the other hand, the stupid and subnormal are moved much more directly by instincts and emotions. Their lack of imagination, poor perceptions and want of reasoning or comparing power, make their self-control weak. In sudden stress or an unusual situation, they are easily swept away and respond directly to instinct and feeling. In short the urge of the primitive through the long history of the race cannot be modified sufficiently by the new structure that civilization has built around more intelligent people.

The various distinctions between the feeble-minded and the normal must not be taken with too much confidence. As the motives that govern man are understood, it is easy to see that intelligence is a strong factor in regulating behavior. When it is seen also that at least the larger part of the inmates of prisons are subnormal and at the same time without property or education, it is evident that all these handicaps are dominating causes of conduct. This position is made still more certain by the further evidence that nearly all of the repeaters in prison are of this type.

Most states already make some allowances in their criminal codes for the defective and the insane. This is really an acknowledgment that the activity of the human machine is governed by its make and environment. The history of the treatment of the insane serves to show the uncertainty of all man's theories as to punishment and responsibility. Doubtless at a very early age in the history of man it was discovered that there were people who acted so abnormally that they could not be classified with the great mass. Such persons were supposed to be possessed of devils or demons, and various incantations and practices were used to drive the devils out. Failing in this they were put in prison, loaded with chains or put to death because of their danger to the community.

In other communities, however, insane persons were thought to be possessed of special gifts. God had come nearer to them than to common mortals, and they were seers or prophets endowed with a portion of the divine power.

Either view of the problem is explainable by the lack of scientific or exact knowledge that marks early societies. Still these societies relied on punishments just as much as our present law-makers and enforcers, possibly more, because presumably less enlightened. Further investigation and experiences with the insane have convinced even the most casual observer that they function somewhat differently from other people; there is not the same certainty between stimulus and response. What they will do and how they will act under given conditions cannot be foretold with anything approaching the exactness that is possible with the normal.

The origin of the insanity in many cases is clearly traceable: sometimes to lesions; sometimes to illness; sometimes to the mode of life; perhaps more is due to heredity than to any other cause. At any rate in theory the civilized world has long since ceased to hold the insane criminally responsible for their acts. This applies only to the clearly insane. The border-line is impossible to find, and many cases are so difficult to classify that there is often a doubt as to where the given patient belongs. In times when the crowd is mad with the mob psychology of hatred, people are impatient of insanity and do not care whether the accused was sane or not at the time of the commission of the act. Many insane are put to death or sentenced to long terms of punishments. Jails and other penal institutions are constantly sorting their inmates and finding many who were clearly insane at the time their sentences began.

Society is beginning to find out that even where there is no marked insanity, many are so near idiocy that they cannot fairly be held responsible for their acts. The line here is just as vague and uncertain as with the insane. Thus far, society has not provided adequate protection for the public against this class; neither has it properly cared for these unfortunates. It has simply excused their conduct, except in cases where some act is so shocking that it arouses special hatred, and then it freely declares that it makes no difference whether the accused is a defective or not; he is of no value to the world and should die. Many of this class are put to death. I am inclined to think that most of those executed are either insane or serious defectives; and those who say that such people are of no value are probably right. It is perhaps equally true that few if any are of value, for when value is considered we are met with the question: "Value to whom, or for what?" All you can say of any one is that he wishes to live, and has the same inherent instincts and emotions toward life as are common to all other men.

Even the legal tests as to insanity and feeble-mindedness are neither logical nor humane. Often the definition is given by courts that if one is able to distinguish between right and wrong, he is sane within the meaning of the law. This definition of insanity is utterly unscientific. If the insane or the defective above an idiot is questioned specifically whether certain distinct things are right or wrong, he can generally give the conventional classification. Often he can tell much better than the intelligent man, for he has been arbitrarily taught the things that are right and wrong and has not the originality or ability to inquire whether the classification is right or how far circumstances and conditions determine right and wrong.

Conduct is ruled by emotion, and actions depend not upon whether one has learned to classify certain conduct as right or wrong, but whether from education, life or otherwise, the thought of a certain act produces a quick and involuntary reaction against doing it. No one believes or feels that it is always really wrong to violate some statutes, and most men indulge in many practices that are wrong and repulsive but not forbidden by the criminal code.

Furthermore, the insane and subnormal are influenced by punishment and fear. Even the animal responds to both. It is possible that in many instances those who are insane and subnormal are influenced by fear more than the intelligent and normal. The most that can be said is that they have not the same power of resistance that is given stronger men. This means only that they have not stored up the experiences of life so well; that their nervous system has not so well conveyed impressions, or that their power of comparison is less; this, in turn, means that it will take greater stress or harder environment to overcome the inhibitions of the sane than the insane. The treatment of the insane and the defective is an acknowledgment that all conduct comes from a direct response of the machine to certain stimuli and the machine can act only in a way consistent with its mechanism.

In other cases, the courts often recognize the strength of hereditary defects in nullifying environment with its strict ideas of right and wrong. The kleptomaniac is generally recognized as being a well-defined class of the insane. Most of the shop-lifters are women. This is especially a female crime. It is useless to explain why. It is not a daring crime; it is secretive in its nature; it requires more stealth than courage; it especially appeals to women on account of their taste for the finery exhibited at stores. The kleptomaniac, however, is generally a rich or influential woman. She steals something she does not need, and she is therefore held to be a kleptomaniac and not responsible.

The poor woman who steals something she actually needs is not a kleptomaniac. I have no doubt that the rich woman who could not resist shop-lifting is a kleptomaniac. I have just as little doubt that the poor woman, with an imperfect make, found her environment such that she was forced to act as she did. If a rich woman is irresponsible and cannot resist when she steals something she does not need, I can see no reason why a poor woman is not likewise irresponsible when she takes something that she needs or must have. The kleptomaniac finds herself in a position where her emotions and her feelings are too strong for her judgment and inhibitions. Everyone who acts must act from similar causes or inducements. There is no special providence in the realm of mind. There is no room for chance in any natural phenomenon. Possibly the public will understand sometime, and law-makers and law-enforcers will place crime and punishment on a scientific basis.

XXVII

SOCIAL CONTROL

Organizations and cults are forever coining new expressions that sound "pat" and for this reason seem true. As a rule, these terms and phrases are put in the shape of general statements that may or may not mean something; but their "pat" sound is used to justify all sorts of excesses and violations of individual rights. The term "social control" is met everywhere now. It may imply much or little, according to the construction of the users. It is meant at least to imply that somewhere is lodged a power to bring under control or supervision the refractory or evil elements of society for the well being of the whole. As a rule, under this phrase anything is justified which seems in some way fit for the community as a whole. The fact that the restraint interferes with personal liberty seems to have no bearing on the matter. Social control necessarily means that the majority of the members of a social unit shall limit the freedom of action of the individual to conform to its view. Of course, the majority has the right because it has the power. In the discussion of political or philosophical questions, "right" means little more or less than "power." A right must be based upon some custom or habit with some power to enforce it, or it cannot be claimed. It can never be enjoyed without the power to obtain it.

The relation of society to the individual has been one long conflict. This is necessarily true because every human organism has instincts, feelings and desires and is naturally impatient at any limitations placed upon it unless self-imposed. On the other hand, organized society functions to preserve itself, and if the activities of the individual are hostile to this preservation the individual must give way. Theorists of various schools are forever propounding social ideas, with the positive assurance that, if followed, they would work automatically and heal all social ills. But it must be evident that neither from history nor philosophy can any such theory be proved. Between the extreme anarchistic view that each person should be free of control by law, and the extreme socialistic view of an extension of state organization until all property and all industrial activity shall be administered by the state and collectively owned, social life in its relation to the individual is always shifting. No one can find the proper line, and if there were a line it would forever change. On the one hand, the power of the strongest element in social organization is always seeking to enlarge the province of the state. On the other hand, the individual unit following the natural instincts for its development is reaching out for more freedom and life. When the theorists in each camp manage to push so hard that both can no longer be maintained, the old organization of society breaks up into new units, immediately to re-form in some new way.

This struggle of contending forces is a prolific and unavoidable source of crime. When organized society goes too far, the individual units rebel and clash with law; when the units swing too far away from the social organization and defy the power of the state, almost automatically some sort of a new organization becomes the state. Whether this new one discards all old forms and laws and acts without the written law, is of no concern. It at least acts and sets limits to the individual life. If it were possible for all legislative bodies to meet and repeal all laws, the state would still remain; the people would live and automatically form themselves into a certain order and protect that order either by written law or vigilance committees. At least the people would act together.

The majority generally has some religious creed, and to it this is all important. This creed is made up of observances, such as holy days, the support of the prevailing religion, the condemnation of witchcraft and magic, and the like. These and other doctrines often have been enforced upon those who have no faith in the regulations. The enforcement of such laws in the past has been by the most drastic penalties and has brought extreme suffering upon the world. No religious organization has ever seemed willing to confine its activities to propaganda, teaching and moral suasion; those methods are too slow, and the evils and consequences of disbelief are too great. Laws of this drastic character are still part of the penal codes of various states and nations, and well-organized bodies are always strenuously seeking to extend the application of such laws and re-enact at least a portion of the religious code that has been outgrown.

Individuals have likewise found, or at least believed, that certain personal habits were best for them, for instance, abstaining from alcohol and tobacco in all forms. Not content with propaganda, they have sought to force their views upon others, many of whom deeply resent their interference.

It is not enough that certain things shall be best for the health and physical welfare of a community. This does not justify the wise law-giver in making them a part of the penal code. If so, the code would be very long. No doubt coffee and tea, and perhaps meat, are injurious to health. Most likely the strength of the community would be conserved if regular sleeping hours were kept and if great modifications or changes were made in dress. But this does not justify criminal statutes. The code must take notice of something more than the general welfare. Unless the end sought to be attained is very direct and plain and the evil great so that a large majority believes in the law, it should be left to education and to other voluntary social forces.

A large part of the community has always attributed many criminal acts to intoxicating drinks. I am convinced that with such crimes as murder, burglary, robbery, forgery and the like, alcohol has had little to do. Petty things, like disorderly conduct, are often caused by intoxicating liquor, and these land a great many temporarily in jail, but these acts are really not criminal. Men have been temporarily locked up for over-drinking. If over-eating had been treated the same as over-drinking, the jails would often be filled with gluttons. As to health, probably the glutton takes the greater chance. A very large percentage of deaths would have been materially delayed except for excessive eating. The statements ascribing crime to intoxicating drinks have generally been made by those who are obsessed with a hatred of alcohol. As a rule if one lands in prison and has not been a total abstainer, his downfall is charged to rum. Statistics have been gathered in prison often by chaplains who, in the main, are prohibitionists and interested in sustaining an opinion. The facts are mainly furnished by inmates of prisons, a poor source from which to gather facts and draw deductions, especially as to the cause of crime. Prisoners are interested in only one thing, and that is getting out. They understand perfectly well what kind of statistics the chaplain wants and these are given. It is the nature and part of the protective instinct of everyone to find some excuse for his acts. Alcohol has always furnished this excuse. It is a good alibi; it is readily believed, always awakens sympathy and at once turns the wrath of a provincial community from the inmate of the prison to the saloon-keeper.

Even if prisoners were unlike others and wished to tell the truth about themselves, they have not the art and understanding to give the causes of their plight. No man, however intelligent, can do this, least of all one of inferior brain power, little education and not trained in dealing with facts. The prison inmate, like everyone else, knows only that he followed what seemed to him the line of least resistance, and that every step in his course was preceded by another and that there was a reason for what he did. Most likely he does not know the reason. In the hours of his despair he goes over his life in every detail, at every crossroad, and at all the forks where paths branch, always wishing he had gone the other way.

While this is true, he could know neither the dangers that lurked along other roads, nor the fact that he had no choice about the way he went. All he knows is that he stumbled along a certain path which led to disaster. All the paths of life lead to tragedy; it is only a question as to how and when. With some, the evil day is longer delayed and the disaster seems not so hard to bear.

In a sense, all the classifications as to the cause of crime are misleading and worthless. Your existence is the result of infinite chances and causes appalling in their number. Out of a thousand eggs, one is fertilized by perhaps one of a billion sperms, and from this you have been given life. Each of your parents and grandparents and so on, back for two hundred thousand years of human ancestors, and back to infinity before man was born, was the result of the same seemingly blind and almost impossible hazard. The infinitely microscopic chance that each of us had for life cannot be approximated. All the drops of water in the ocean, or all the grains of sand upon the shore, or all the leaves on all the trees, if converted into numbers and used as a denominator, with one for a numerator, could hardly tell the fraction of a chance that gave us life.

The causes of human action are infinite, and no cause stands isolated from the rest. In the first place we cannot tell the meaning of the word "cause" when applied to a problem of this sort. In law the ordinary rule for a "proximate cause" is "an event or happening in the direct line of causation, not too remote, that has led to the result, and without which the result could not have happened." But this means nothing. Infinite are the causes which have led to every act, and without each one of the infinite causes the act could not have resulted. If it be something that affected a life, and had it not happened then the life would have drifted somewhere else. In the end it would have reached the same harbor of Nirvana. But the life would not have been the same. A drop of water falls on the Rocky Mountains, it trickles along, going around through pebbles and grains of sand; it joins with others, meets trees and roots, winds and twists perhaps for hundreds, even thousands of miles before one can tell by what channel it will reach the sea. Infinite accidents determine even which sea it shall finally reach. The most radical advocates of social control are never at a loss to lay their fingers on causes or to know what would have happened if something else had not happened; they never hesitate to forbid seemingly innocent acts because they are certain that evil will follow. They are contemptuous of one who wants to preserve the semblance and spirit of freedom.

Life has none too much to offer where men are

left to control themselves, and to be forbidden to follow your inclinations and desires because sometimes they may result disastrously, is to give up what seems to be a substance for what is most likely a shadow.

All we can tell about the man whom we are pleased to call a criminal, is that he had a poor equipment and met certain influences, motives and conditions, called environment, on his journey. We know that at a given time the journey has reached a certain point; it has met disaster or success, or most likely indifference. At a certain point he has reached a prison or is waiting for the hangman to tie a noose around his neck. Is heredity responsible? We know of many who apparently started out with an equipment no better. These may be business men and congressmen and deacons in the church. While we do not know and cannot know the trend and relative strength of the instincts in the various machines or the emotions that these and the whole equipment produced, apparently an equipment as poor as that of the criminal has met success, or at least kept its possessor out of jail. Was it then his environment? We have known men placed in the same environment, perhaps a brother, conquering difficulties and bringing success from what seemed to promise certain defeat. Why did one fail where the other conquered? Was it the "will" that caused one to be the "captain of his soul"? What then is the "will" and who gave the weak will to one and the strong will to another? And, if each was born with a certain "will" or the capacity to make a certain "will," who then is responsible for the result? Or, does the word "will" mean anything, as usually applied?

All we can tell is that a certain equipment met a certain environment, and the result was early disaster. A change of even the slightest factor of environment might have saved the victim from hanging, so that he could die a respectable and peaceful death from tuberculosis or cancer.

After all, the inevitable tragedy that in some form marks the end is not so important as the sensations and experiences that one meets on the road. Life is hopeless and colorless indeed if these experiences are chosen for the wayfarer and the sensations are enforced or denied, as the case may be. Nothing recompenses the individual for the denial of his chance to follow his own path.

XXVIII

INDUSTRIALISM AND CRIME

It was not until about the middle of the eighteenth century that the desire for the creation and accumulation of property began to rule the world. Up to that time such small amounts of property as man needed or coveted had either been produced in a simple manner by himself or taken in the easiest way.

This new passion has made a large part of the modern criminal code. A world of warriors, religious zealots and pastoral people could not readily adapt themselves to the change. Criminal codes were lengthened; methods of getting property and keeping it were provided for, and other ways condemned. It must be obvious that it was not easy for man with his age-old machine, his inherited institutions and his ancient folk-ways, to adjust himself rapidly to the change. New conditions and laws created new criminals.

With the growth of the factory system and accelerated industrial development, an overweening desire for material things was awakened. As neither individuals nor societies can be possessed of more than one overpowering emotion at a time, the devotion to property naturally weakened religious fervor. Religion became more an abstract belief and a social organization than a vital thing affecting life and conduct. Even before this time there was growing up in the world a protest against the religious superstition that had led to the cruelties of the past. The scientist and the modern philosopher were making their contributions to the world of thought, and these contributions were slowly affecting life and conduct.

A doubt of old creeds and doctrines and faiths was coming over the minds of men. Social conventions were loosening, new customs and habits were becoming folk-ways. In short, society and life were growing more fluid and adaptable. The growth of property holdings created new desires and new temptations. The accumulation of large fortunes brought envy and hatred and ambition. The rise of industries built the large cities, with palaces on one hand and hovels on the other. The vast inequality of wealth and the growth of workers' organizations, together with the spirit of skepticism which activity always brings, caused large numbers to doubt the justice of property rights, the utility of many institutions and the possibility of radical change by social organization. It is perfectly evident that all of this movement brought more conflict between social units, a constant lengthening of the criminal code to protect the interests of the controlling powers, an increase of prisons, and an apparent if not a real increase of crime.

Nothing but a strong government can long endure great inequality of wealth or social condition. The slaves of the past civilization were kept in subjection by main strength and fear. This enslavement was aided by the deep ignorance of the masses who had no means of information and nothing but vague feelings of the injustice of their lot. Even then the poor sometimes revolted, but such outbreaks were generally easily put down by the sword. The growth of political power and industrial independence has been accompanied by the constant conflict of social forces. This means conflict with the law, and the law has always taken its toll of victims.

New inventions and methods that bring power of any sort carry with them social clashes, protests, bitterness, conflicts and violations of law. The invention of gun-powder was the source of great conflict and still continues to add to the inmates of prisons. From the first, the far-reaching effects of high explosives were seen by the wise, and firearms were permitted only in the hands of those who could be depended upon to support the state. Gradually through the needs of the rulers in war they were given to the poor. When the American

Revolution separated us from Great Britain, the spirit of democracy and revolt was strong in the world. A body of peasants had gained independence over the strongest nation on earth. This body, through its delegates, provided in the Constitution of the United States that the people should never be forbidden to bear arms. The cheap production of firearms placed them in the hands of all who wished to buy. This aided feuds and brawls. It also gave strength to the burglar and robber.

America was fast becoming a manufacturing and commercial nation. The accumulation of property was greater, and the inequalities perhaps more marked than in any other land; likewise the poor were more independent. Gradually we came to rely more and more upon the power of law and the force that goes with it to preserve the old order. Legislatures and city councils all over the United States began to limit and forbid carrying firearms. The Constitution of the United States was held no impediment to this legislation. Gradually laws have forbidden the carrying of guns by the common man, and these laws are growing stronger every year. In many states robbery with a gun may mean life imprisonment, while the mere carrying of a revolver is a serious offense. The passage of these drastic laws and the number of prison inmates confined for these offenses show that the invention and use of firearms has affected crime, and likewise that the government is constantly growing more doubtful of the common man.

Civilization largely has to do with the creation and protection of property. Although it is related to literature, architecture, politics, art and the like; even these things if not actually rooted in property are stimulated or affected by property. Civilization has created new crimes and new ways to commit crime. It has likewise created many wants and desires that furnish the motive power of property crimes. Each new invention of civilization adds to these needs and these desires, increases the power of committing crime, and necessitates stricter measures to prevent it. Civilization has likewise created many new outlets for the emotions, strengthened old ones, weakened others and added to the complexity of life. It has imposed added strain and stress upon man's nervous system and through this has caused the abnormalities and excesses that are either crimes or lead to crimes.

Civilization has created the big cities; in other words, the powers and forces that made civilization have made the big cities. The invention and development of the railroad has taken men from the air and sunlight and comparative freedom of motion of the country and the small village, and placed them in an atmosphere not really fitted for normal animal life, especially the life of the young. It has likewise stimulated crime by offering the opportunities and making the suggestions that are potent factors in crime. In country and village life everyone was known, the smallest detail of every life was an open book. This fact furnished a moral restraint to the individual and likewise made it hard for him to violate the rules of the game. The opportunities for collecting large numbers of people who might encourage each other with their conversation and association were very few in rural life. The man who would violate the law must do it alone. Not only this, but he must take his first steps almost without suggestion or aid. This confined criminal conduct largely to the feeble-minded and the seriously defective, and even these could generally live in a country atmosphere where life is simple and easy, without serious danger to themselves or others.

The great city with its swarms of people, its wealth and poverty, its unhealthy atmosphere, its opportunities for everyone to have many associates and still be lost to the community at large, makes irregular lives not only easy, but almost necessary to large numbers of men. Civilization has no doubt created crime as it has created luxury, wealth, refinement and ease. Much luxury has always led to deterioration and decay and is doubtless leading that way now.

One of the latest products of civilization that has had a marked effect on crime is the automobile.

Stringent laws are on the statute books of all states against stealing automobiles, yet stealing and selling automobiles is a flourishing and growing business. A large percentage of the boys in the juvenile courts of our cities are there for stealing automobiles. Yet this is the work of a very short period. I do not mean to say that many of the boys brought into court for stealing automobiles would not have committed some other crime, if automobiles had not been invented and come into general use, but I feel quite sure that many of them are victims of the automobile madness alone.

The automobile is one of the latest manias and fashions that civilization has provided. Almost no one is free from the disease. Conservative business men must have motor cars; clerks and salaried people who cannot afford them must get them; mechanics and professional men who have no need for them, except that others use them, must contrive to buy them. Automobiles are much more important today than houses. Men go into debt and struggle for money to buy gasoline so that they may drive somewhere for the sake of coming back. It has created a psychology all its own, a psychology of movement, of impatience, of waste, of futility. Men in Chicago start to drive to Milwaukee without the slightest reason for going there; they travel the road so fast that they could get no idea of the scenery even if there were something to see.

They hurry as if going for a doctor. They reach their destination and then start back home. The specific desire that is satisfied by this expense and waste is a new one, an emotion of no value in the life processes and probably of great injury in life development. It is a craze for movement, for haste, for what seems like change.

The automobile has made its list of criminals, and it is making them every day. Probably it will continue to make them until the flying machine is perfected, and then to some extent at least the airplane will take its place.

The truth is that man is not adapted to the automobile. His reactions are too simple; his inherent needs are not adjusted to the new life; he has not been built up with barriers to protect him from this insidious temptation which is claiming its victims by the hundreds every day.

The boy is perfectly helpless in the presence of this lure. He wants to do what others do. He is by nature active and venturesome and needs to keep on the move. The mechanism itself appeals to him. He wants to work in a garage. He is anxious to be a chauffeur. He cannot resist an automobile. No such temptation should be placed before a boy. It has added a great deal to the responsibility of parents and teachers, and so far they seem not to have been able to meet that responsibility in any way. Aside from the boys' thefts it has played a great part in crime. The doctor, the real estate agent, the business man cannot afford to be without automobiles. No more can the burglar, the hold-up man, the bank robber, if he would keep up to date. The automobile has raised the robbery of country banks from a vagrant crime, infrequent and dangerous, to a steady occupation coupled with a great deal of excitement and some chance for profit. So far no one has ever suggested anything to counteract or lessen the evil effects except to increase penalties. The crimes committed with and for automobiles are a result of the conditions of life. Out of a thousand men and boys, a certain percentage must commit these crimes just as a certain percentage must die of tuberculosis. The temptation is very great. The human equipment is not strong enough in many people to withstand the temptation. They either buy them when they cannot afford to own them, or they steal them, and either way leads to disaster. No doubt men will some time become adjusted to the automobile as they have become adjusted to the horse, but until that time comes, it will demand its heavy toll of unfortunates.

Not only, it seems to me, does the growth of civilization mean the growth of crime, but that civilization likewise leads to decay. The world has seen the result over and over again, but it cannot learn. Man is an animal; the law of his being demands that he shall live close to nature; he needs the outdoors, the country, the air; he needs to walk and run; otherwise his digestive apparatus will fail, his brain power will decay, and the strength of his legs will be impaired. Civilization runs too much to stomach and nerves, and Nature will have revenge. To be sure, the professional American rhapsodist points out that we are immune from natural law because we have a chance to vote for presidents once in every four years. But there are ample signs that Nature knows little about political institutions or other man-made devices and that she will have her way.

How much the natural limitations of man will permit him to learn and understand; how far his instincts and emotional nature would allow him to be controlled by knowledge, if he had it; what would be the results to life if reason could control him, are pertinent questions that affect all discussion and which may never be satisfactorily answered. It is entirely possible that the student who tries to point out better ways and teach better methods does it only to satisfy his own emotions and is often conscious that it does nothing else. But, whatever the inducing cause or result, given a brain and nervous system and the material that civilization furnishes for reflection, these and other important subjects will be interesting topics of study and furnish material for the reflective powers of man.

XXIX

WAR AND CRIME

All natural phenomena affect the activities of man. It has been repeatedly observed that the number of crimes of assault and murder increases in the summer months and fluctuates with extreme heat or a cooler temperature. The nervous system of man is responsive to all sorts of physical and psychological influences, and criminologists take these into account in considering crime, as doctors take them into account in treating disease. Man is influenced by substantially all the things that affect other structures and by many things that do not. His nervous system is more delicate, his emotional nature more complex, and his brain permits the handling of impressions in a way not possible to lower organisms.

The effect of war has always been manifest in human conduct. Man acts largely from habit and custom; he does as others do, without reflection as to why he should do it or why others do it. War is a sudden, violent and spectacular destroyer of all established habits. In its conduct and preparation it has rules of its own which have no analogy in civil life. The battlefield is a reversion to the primitive; a reversion which man finds it easy to make, for it appeals to fundamental instincts which civilization holds in leash with great difficulty and never with entire success. War especially appeals to the young. Their desire for activity, their impatience with restraint, their love of the spectacular, their untrained emotions, all find a ready outlet in war. Even those who are too young to fight still read of it, talk of it, play at it to the exclusion of other games. War is a profound and rapid maker of mental attitudes and of complexes that are quick to develop and slow to pass away. Both the quick development and slow decay are probably due to the fact that war meets a decided response in the primitive nature of man.

Nearly all the newspapers of America are now calling attention to the increase of crime since the close of the Great War. It is a topic of pulpit and platform discussion. Wild appeals are made for convictions and extreme penalties. Governors and boards of pardon and parole are urged to refuse clemency to prisoners and are roundly condemned when they do their plain duty, even though they do it very reluctantly and tardily.

It is probably true that the close of the war has shown a large increase in criminality, especially in crimes of violence. This is true not only of America but of all European countries. In some of the most afflicted ones civil government for a time has virtually broken down. Both the great need for food and clothing and the overthrowing of conventions, customs and habits are responsible for the change. Here we perceive a notable example of the almost instantaneous disruption of established folk-ways.

For more than four years most of the western world did nothing but kill. The whole world talked of slaughter and devoted its energy to killing. Every sentiment of humanity was forgotten. Even religious ties and religious commands were ignored. The prayers to the Almighty contained requests that He help the various fighting nations to kill their enemies. Everyone was taught to hate. The leaders in the war knew that boys could not do efficient killing unless they learned to fear and hate. The most outrageous falsehoods were freely circulated by every nation about its enemies and their conduct of the war. The highest rewards were offered for new and more efficient ways to kill. Every school was turned over to hate and preparation for war, and, of course, all the churches joined in the universal craze. God would not only forgive killing but reward those who were the most expert at the game.

The newspapers carried stories of battles every day, the dead and wounded often running into the tens of thousands. None of the reports was exact.

Nothing was true. Everything was wild and exaggerated. Facts were not strong enough to make an impression. Lies were deliberately circulated to help the cause.

Every tradition and habit of life was broken and broken all the time. The commandment, "Thou shalt not kill," was repealed. Property was not only ruthlessly destroyed but openly confiscated. Lying was a fine art. When this bears a harvest after the war, the public loudly clamors for hanging boys whose psychology is a direct result of long and intensive training by the leaders of the world.

One life is not worth considering in the face of the holocaust that has taken its hundreds of thousands and has been defended in the schools and churches. It is not strange that the after-war harvest of crimes should come largely from boys, often those boys who did their part on the field of battle. Whether they got the psychology from killing or reading or hearing or playing soldier or training makes no difference. Everyone who has any reasoning power knows that they got it, that it was deliberately given to them if not forced upon them, and that just as deliberately the state is killing them because they took it.

It is not alone the young who show this psychology of killing that has grown out of the war. Organized society, the public, juries, judges, pardon boards and governors, show that war has made them cruel and wanton of human life. The great number of hangings since the war is patent to all observers. In normal times juries were very loath to pronounce the death penalty. With any possible excuse they always saved life. Now they pride themselves on taking life. Even insanity does not always prevent an execution.

Numerous are the evidences of the derangements the war has created and left behind. A few years ago a prize fight would not have been permitted in more than one or two states in the Union. Now state after state is passing laws to permit prize fights to take place, and even the best society has given its sanction to this sort of sport. Whether the state should permit prize fights is not the question. The fact is, as everyone knows, that it is permitted on account of a psychology growing out of the war. We content ourselves with saying it will never do to raise our boys as molly-coddles; they must learn to fight.

It is not alone murder that can be traced directly to the war psychology. Robbery and burglary have rapidly increased, and much of this is due to the emotions of boys. The robbing of country banks has grown to be almost a pastime, and often one or more participants in these raids is a returned soldier.

What should be done to meet these new conditions? Common honesty, common sense and common humanity alike plainly show that a large part of the crimes of violence are due to the war. Will hangings and life sentences stop them? And, if so, is it right for organized society to ignore its responsibility and place it on the young men that they innoculated with the universal madness? It is expecting too much to think that there is any process by which society can be made to think and feel. Some day, however, when the war fever passes away crime will again take its normal place.

This phenomenon is not new in the world. Everyone interested has noted it before. It has followed all great wars. War means the breaking up of old habits, the destruction of many inhibitions, which in the strongest civilization are only skin deep at the best. It means the return to the primitive feelings that once ruled man.

The Napoleonic Wars left a long heritage of crime. Every nation in Europe was affected by them. Many years passed before the world grew tranquil. Our Civil War brought its harvest of crime. It was felt both North and South. It was not confined to homicide but was shown in all sorts of criminal statistics, especially crimes of violence.

I do not write as a pacifist. There is nothing in the constitution of man that makes pacifism anything but a dream. Man is largely ruled by fear and hate, and it is not possible to imagine an individual or a race that under sufficient provocation will not fight. Neither is it possible that nations will not always, from time to time, find the provocation sufficiently great. Individuals and nations can philosophize and reason and make compromises when they are calm; but let them be moved by fear and hatred, and these emotions will sweep away every other feeling. The conditions for war were ripe in 1914, and it was inevitable that America should be in it too. This should not make one wish for war nor believe in war nor close one's eyes to its horrors and results. Much less should it prevent him from trying to do his part to restore sanity to the world.

Another consequence of war which America is passing through is the spirit of super-patriotism. This is always aroused and must be aroused to carry on the war. It is potent in creating the psychology that makes men fight. Every people teaches that its own country is the best; that its laws and institutions excel those of all other lands. This spirit is taken advantage of and used by designing men. It is used to send to jail those who criticise existing things. It is used to hamper and destroy any effort to change laws and institutions. The one who criticises conditions is a disturber and a traitor. Those who profit by existing things are always intense patriots and by means of cheap appeals and trite expressions seek to stifle discussion and criticism. This war has borne a deadly harvest of restrictive legislation in America. We are no longer an asylum for political offenders. We no longer stand for freedom of speech. Old traditions and constitutional and legal guarantees have been swept aside under the hysteria which has prevailed during and since the war. These results were inevitable and will follow war as long as man is man.

All the after-effects of the World War show how completely man is ruled by forces over which he has no control. If considerable numbers of the people have been moved by war hysteria, and if a large part of crime is directly traceable to war, it seems plain that all human action could be traced to some controlling cause, if only man could be wise enough and industrious and humane enough to find the cause. It is plain that the law of cause and effect influences mental phenomena as it does physical acts, and sometime, perhaps, men will seek to avoid the effect by removing the cause.

XXX

CIVILIZATION AND CRIME

As children we have all amused ourselves by looking into a kaleidoscope, turning it around and around and watching the changing patterns formed from the mixing bits of different colored glass in the other end. Each turn makes a different pattern and each bit of glass seems to seek a spot in the general medley where it can be settled until another turn drives it to find a resting place somewhere else. The organization of individual units into a group is more or less such a formation, each seeking to adjust itself to a pattern and finding that the pattern is ever-changing and the individual units obliged to seek new positions and make new adjustments.

It is vain for social theorists to talk of a perfect order, a system of social organization that will find the proper place for each unit and bring social symmetry out of the whole. Such a society is not consistent with the varied capacities and wants of men. Neither is a perfect order possible with ever-changing and moving physical forces, with new mental conceptions, with new needs and wants, with constant births and deaths, and with the innate instincts of man.

Some system may be the best for a time but must in turn give place to new formations. In this process the old is ever mixed with the new. The past hangs on to plague the present, and the vision of the future disturbs the quiet and stability that the present inherited from the past. Organizations of society are necessary and automatic. The frost on the window pane takes its pattern, the crystals in the glass and stone have their formations, the grain of sand, the plant—all forms of animal life—the solar system and, doubtless, an infinite number of other systems which the eye cannot see or the mind comprehend take on form and order. The symmetry and shape of any of these organizations may be shattered by growth or catastrophe, and new forms may take their place. All life is constant friction and constant adjustment, each particle in a blind way trying to find a more harmonious relation, but never reaching complete rest.

The social and political patterns that men have taken have been of many forms. All through the past these have changed, and the laws and habits that were meant to hold men together, have been made and discarded as fast as new emotions or ideas have gained the power to make the change.

Men are of all degrees of adaptability. Some can readily conform to the new. Some adjust themselves very slowly. Man's structure is fixed; his inherent instincts are of ancient origin, always urging him to primitive reactions; his habits are slowly formed and slowly changed. Slowly he settles himself to the conditions that surround him. He learns their demands; he manages to conform, but the folk-ways that he knew and the way of life he learned must be changed to something else. Every new adjustment, every change of organization, every modification made by civilization, bears its toll of victims who have not been able to adjust themselves to the new order.

The first criminal regulations, doubtless, had to do with the personal relations of men. The number of offenses was small for life was simple, wants were few, and ambition rare. The growth of religion created a ferocious criminal code, regulating every thought and action that God's agents thought might offend the Deity or threaten their power on earth. Anyone interested in the story of punishment for heresy, sorcery or other crimes growing out of religious fanaticism, can read the story in Lecky's *History of Rationalism in Europe,* in White's *A History of the Warfare of Science with Theology in Christendom,* in Draper's *Intellectual Development of Europe,* and in many other books. The Spanish Inquisition alone furnished about 350,000 victims in the two centuries of its power. Many of them were burned alive, many others were killed by the most cruel torture that could be devised by man. Up to recent times more victims have been put to death for heresy and kindred crimes against religion than for any other cause. Next to this no doubt stand political crimes. Even America hanged old women for witchcraft, a crime they could not commit. Practically all the victims of religious and political persecution have been guiltless of any real crimes, and among them were always many of the noblest of their age.

Every general change of religious or political ideas bears its quota of crimes. For whatever the religious or political organization, it always uses every means in its power to perpetuate itself. This is as true of republics as of monarchies, although the severity of punishment and the amount of heresy permitted change from time to time. Each age is sure that it has the true religion and the God-given political organization. In every age the accepted religion is true, and the king and the state can do no wrong.

One thing only seems to be sure. Human nature does not change. Whether it was the theological systems of the ancient world fighting to keep Christianity out, or Christianity fighting to preserve itself, the same cruel, bigoted, fanatical majority has been found to do its will, and the same reasons and excuses have served the law from the earliest times down to today.

A letter of the younger Pliny, who was then governor of Bythinia-Pontus, a province of Rome, asking the Emperor Trajan for instructions in dealing with the early Christians shows how persistent are intolerance and bigotry. This might have been written yesterday to seek advice in the suppression of opinion and punishment for sedition in any of the most advanced governments of the modern world, as it was in the most advanced of the ancient world. The letter is here reproduced as an interesting exhibit of human nature and it fixity.

Pliny, the younger, was born in 61 A.D. and became governor of the province of Bythinia-Pontus about the year 112 A.D. under the Emperor Trajan. In the discharge of his duties as governor, Pliny discovered that the conversion of many of his subjects to Christianity had resulted in a falling off of trade in the victims usually purchased for sacrifices at the temples and in other commodities used in connection with pagan worship. As a good governor, Pliny sought to remedy this economic situation, and his plan was to restore his subjects to their old forms of worship. Thus he was brought into contact with Christianity. The following letters, one from Pliny to Trajan, and the other, Trajan's reply, show the situation. These documents are from the Tenth Book of Pliny's Correspondence, Letters 97 and 98.

PLINY ASKING INSTRUCTIONS OF TRAJAN ON TRIALS OF CHRISTIANS

It is my invariable rule, Sir, to refer to you in all matters where I feel doubtful; for who is more capable of removing my scruples, or informing my ignorance? Having never been present at any trials concerning those who profess Christianity, I am unacquainted not only with the nature of their crimes, or the measure of their punishment, but how far it is proper to enter into an examination concerning them. Whether, therefore, any difference is usually made with respect to ages, or no distinction is to be observed between the young and the adult; whether repentance entitles them to a pardon; or if a man has been once a Christian, it avails nothing to desist from his error; whether the very profession of Christianity, unattended with any criminal act, or only the crimes themselves inherent in the profession are punishable; on all these points I am in great doubt. In the meanwhile, the method I have observed towards those who have been brought before me as Christians is this: I asked them whether they were Christians; if they admitted it, I repeated the question twice, and threatened them with punishment; if they persisted, I ordered them to be at once punished: for I was persuaded, whatever the nature of their opinions might be, a contumacious and inflexible obstinacy certainly deserved correction.

There were others also brought before me possessed with the same infatuation, but being Roman citizens, I directed them to be sent to Rome. But this crime spreading (as is usually the case) while it was actually under prosecution, several instances of the same nature occurred. An anonymous information was laid before me, containing a charge against several persons, who upon examination denied they were Christians, or had ever been so. They repeated after me an invocation to the gods, and offered religious rites with wine and incense before your statue (which for that purpose I had ordered to be brought, together with those of the gods), and even reviled the name of Christ: whereas there is no forcing, it is said, those who are really Christians into any of these compliances: I thought it proper, therefore, to discharge them. Some among those who were accused by a witness in person at first confessed themselves Christians, but immediately after denied it: the rest owned indeed that they had been of that number formerly, but had now (some above three, others more, and a few above twenty years ago) renounced that error. They all worshipped your statue and the images of the gods, uttering imprecations at the same time against the name of Christ. They affirmed the whole of their guilt, or their error, was, that they met on a stated day before it was light, and addressed a form of prayer to Christ, as to a divinity, binding themselves by a solemn oath, not for the purposes of any wicked design, but never to commit any fraud, theft, or adultery, never to falsify their word, nor deny a trust when they should be called upon to deliver it up; after which it was their custom to separate, and then re-assemble, to eat in common a harmless meal. From this custom, however, they desisted after the publication of my edict, by which, according to your commands, I forbade the meeting of any assemblies.

After receiving this account, I judged it so much the more necessary to endeavor to extort the real truth, by putting two female slaves to the torture, who were said to officiate in their religious rites: but all I could discover was evidence of an absurd and extravagant superstition. I deemed it expedient, therefore, to adjourn all further proceedings, in order to consult you. For it appears to be a matter highly deserving your consideration, more especially as great numbers must be involved in the danger of these prosecutions, which have already extended, and are still likely to extend, to persons of all ranks and ages, and even of both sexes. In fact, this contagious superstition is not confined to the cities only, but has spread its infection among the neighboring villages and country. Nevertheless, it still seems possible to restrain its progress. The temples, at least, which were once almost deserted, begin now to be frequented; and the sacred rites, after a long intermission, are again revived; while there is a general demand for the victims, which till lately found very few purchasers. From all this it is easy to conjecture what numbers might be reclaimed if a general pardon were granted to those who shall repent of their error.

TRAJAN TO PLINY

You have adopted a right course, my dearest Secundus, in investigating the charges against the Christians who were brought before you. It is not possible to lay down any general rule for all such cases. Do not go out of your way to look for them. If indeed they should be brought before you, and the crime is proved, they must be punished; with the restriction, however, that where the party denies he is a Christian, and shall make it evident that he is not, by invoking our gods, let him (notwithstanding any former suspicion) be pardoned upon his repentance. Anonymous information ought not to be received in any sort of prosecution. It is introducing a very dangerous precedent, and is quite foreign to the spirit of our age.

Civilization is largely a question of new machinery and methods. It is not the humanizing of men. It is plain that no matter what the time or age, the characteristics of man remain the same. His structure does not change; his emotional life cannot change. New objects and desires may control his feeling, but whatever the aim of the age and place, the same inherent emotions control.

Intolerance has been one of the great sources of evil all down the ages. It is practically certain that neither time nor education has made man more kindly in his judgment of his fellows or more tolerant in his opinions and life. All that education can do is to remove some of the inducing causes that have always brought the sharp conflicts and awakened the cruelty of man.

Every civilization brings new evils and new complexities which man meets with the same machine and the same emotions. It is fairly certain that no nobler idealism or no finer feelings have been planted or cultivated in man since the dawn of history, and when it is thoroughly realized that man's structure is fixed and cannot be changed it seems as if none could be developed.

XXXI

THE CONVICT

Human nature is so weak and imperfect that, at its best, it needs all the encouragement it can get. The comradeship of friends, and the attitude of the public and acquaintances are of the greatest importance in effecting the development of most lives. Sooner or later the convicted man is turned out either on probation or parole, or at the expiration of his sentence. He was probably none too strong a man before his conviction. His heredity was poor in most cases, and his environment completed his downfall. He faces the world again with a serious handicap that he did not have at first. If he had just recovered from a severe illness, everyone he met would do all he could to help him; his environment would be made easier than before his confinement in the hospital; and especially from the conditions that placed him there, both society and his neighbors would try to see that he should, as far as possible, be saved. If he had been one of those who could live only by means of his own work, and if on account of himself or his family he had been obliged to overstrain, an easier place would probably be found for him. The chances of going to the hospital the second time would be very much less than they were the first time. Even his experience in confinement would be of use, and through that experience he would be taught to live and preserve his health.

The discharged prisoner is met in an entirely different way. The ex-convict is under doubt and suspicion from the start. On the slightest provocation he is reminded of his past. He is always under suspicion unless, perhaps, he professes a change of heart. Such a change implies a physical process which is impossible. Some sudden exaltation may furnish him a new emotion for a time, but this can last only while the stimulus has power to act. It will soon pass away and the man will be himself again. It may be possible that here and there is a nature of such an emotional temperament, that religion or socialism or single tax or some other strong conviction may possess him until such time as his feelings begin to cool and change, when he will be safe. But most men are inherently the same when they come out of prison as when they go in. Under right treatment they may gain a little more wisdom as to life that will help them make adjustments; or they may be relieved from some burdens, or placed in an environment of less stress and strain where it will be easier to live. In those cases, the attitude and help of the community are all-important.

Society is not entirely to blame for looking on him with suspicion. It knows he once failed. It has been taught that this failure was due to a moral delinquency outside the law of cause and effect, and society is naturally suspicious that he will offend again or molest the community in some other way. Had he been confined because he had not the strength to meet his environment; had the law put him in custody under expert control until he gained the strength for his battle with life; or had a new environment been provided under scientific direction as in the case of a hospital patient, society would then take another view and do all it could to help him. New comrades and associates would surround him to show him the way, and they would make his burden lighter. Instead of this, he comes out with his ability to adjust himself to life lessened. If a crime is committed in his community he is blamed or at least suspected. He is known to the police and often "rounded-up." This directly interferes with his employment, places him at a disadvantage with his associates, and drives him into the company of others who feel that the world is against them and that a life of crime is all there is left to follow. It is not hard to see how men come to be "repeaters." It is hard to understand when they do not.

XXXII

ISOLATION AND STERILIZATION

The growing belief that crime comes largely from the subnormal has created a more or less definite demand for the isolation of the moron before the commission of crime and for the sterilization of certain misfits, especially after conviction. Both of these methods are very drastic, and while society must and will adopt any way that seems to be necessary to protect itself, still before accepting such drastic remedies it should be very clear that the danger is sufficiently great to justify the means, that the desired result will follow and that no other means will bring about the end.

In this discussion it should be remembered that the mental classification of children and grown-ups is only in its infancy, that much that is freely stated is still in the realm of theory, and that time and patience in making investigations and classifying facts are most important in arriving at correct results.

The really intelligent are as abnormal as the defective. The great masses of men are rather mediocre, and those above and below are exceptions. This depends on how broad is the class included in the normal. There are no sharp divisions anywhere; above, the normal shades imperceptibly into those of unusual intelligence, and below it fades just as gradually into the sub-normal. While defectives are more apt to commit crimes, in the main this is because their environment is too hard for their machine.

The sub-normal are probably more tractable and less disposed to the emotions that lead to criminal acts than are the more intelligent. Their crimes are especially noticed because they seem to be without any serious motive and often shockingly brutal. City life most readily uncovers the sub-normal. This is true because the strain is far greater in the city than the country. There are exceptions to this rule, particularly those portions of the country that are barren and unproductive territory into which the venturesome and obvious unfits are drawn.

The prisons are not the only places which are inhabited by the sub-normal and the misfit. The hardest and most disagreeable and most poorly paid labor is largely done by this class of people. Very few people of superior intelligence and education do manual labor and the more disagreeable the manual labor, the more certain it is that the job is done by the sub-normal and the misfit. A large part of the farm labor, the odd jobs and common labor in small towns, the cheaper labor on railroads, in factories and all industrial plants is given to this sort of men. In the country and small village, where life is easy, this class seldom makes trouble and is hardly known. These men and women easily and naturally fall into a place in the industry and society of the village and are often among the most useful members.

A general examination of all men to discover the defective and the sub-normal, coupled with a demand that all such be sent to some place of confinement, would meet with such a protest from all classes seriously affected as to end not only the demand but the further agitation of the subject. Any such law, if carried out, would not only seriously increase the cost of all industry, but in many instances would make it impossible to carry it on. It is hardly conceivable that above the idiot, society shall make examinations and tests and confine or sterilize large classes of people who have not yet developed anti social tendencies, but who on account of feeble intellects might sometime commit crime.

The world has ample data at hand to show more humane and at the same time much cheaper ways, even methods that will yield a profit. These ways have been abundantly illustrated by history and can be witnessed in operation every day.

England was repeatedly conquered and settled by brigands and misfits. When her people grew more homogeneous and orderly she sent her anti-social to New Zealand and to Virginia. In New Zealand with its opportunities these outcasts and their descendants prospered and were as orderly and conventional as the English society that banished them for England's good. The colonies in Virginia with access to land and a chance to make homes for themselves established a social order and formed communities more prosperous than the ones that sent them out. Many of their descendants are now successful and important members of every western state.

In fact, most of the European immigrants who have settled in the United States were the poor and the outcast, the misfits of European countries. With better opportunities and a chance to build up homes in a new land, their descendants are at least the equals of those who stayed behind. The growth and development of the United States westward from the Atlantic seaboard has been effected by the poorer and less intelligent, but often the more venturesome, who constantly turned West to get cheaper land and a better chance. The residents of these western states compare very favorably with those who still reside in the sections of the country which these pioneers left behind. It cannot be shown that the less intelligent have criminal natures. All that can be shown is that they have a poorer equipment to meet the stress and strain of life. To make most of this class safe, all that is needed is fairer conditions and an easier environment. If society could only recover from the obsession that what is necessary to regulate man is plenty of prisons and harder punishments, it would be fairly easy and infinitely cheaper to improve the environment from which crime springs than to visit vengeance on the victim.

The effect of education is very great. Many a subnormal and backward person has been educated so he could take a place in life that those with a much greater natural ability could not fill.

Beyond the segregation of the imbecile, the insane and those who have committed crime, it is dangerous to go. The course of preventing crime lies in the other direction, better opportunity and an easier life.

It has grown to be a commonplace in the discussion of crime to speak of isolation and sterilization as the proper treatment of the criminal and defective. This is generally done without any clear understanding of the laws of heredity.

The laws of the transmission from parent to child of traits and tendencies are not yet well enough known to justify any attempt to interfere with the function of life, except in the case of the idiotic. It is plain that crime cannot be inherited. Certain defects in the brain and nervous system can be and are inherited. No brain or nervous system is perfect, so the problem is one of the incapacity which causes the maladjustment. Crime results from defective heredity when applied to the environment. It comes from the inability of the machine to make the necessary adjustments of life. The making of the criminal is largely a question of his fortune or misfortune in the environment where he is placed. It is absurd to say that one inherits the tendency to rob or rape or burglarize or kill. He may inherit an unstable organization that in certain hostile environments will lead him to any of these crimes. For that matter all men inherit the organization that will bring these results if the environment is sufficiently hard. Society may in many ways place too high a value on human life. Still we punish men who place too low a value on the lives of others, and the state should be very slow to destroy life or the capacity for life.

There is much to learn, much to explain about the mysterious workings of heredity, before man can undertake to say that he has the wisdom or justice to choose the ones who should be the bearers of life to the future.

It is most common to find in the same family various degrees of intelligence. Now and then a man of such high powers and faculties is born that he is regarded by scientists as a "sport" who defies all known laws in his origin. Often one person in a family is of commanding strength, while the rest are commonplace.

The insanity and disease that afflict many men of genius is well known. Grasset in his book *The Semi-Insane and the Semi-Responsible* has given a long list of eminent names. Many great authors have depicted insanity in their most gifted characters. Genius is frequently an indication of insanity. It is a wide departure from the normal.

The obscure and lowly origin of many of the world's greatest men seems to point to the fact that Nature has methods that man cannot comprehend and with which it is not wise for him to interfere. The fact is that genius, or even great strength or ability in the parent, is by no means sure to be handed down. In fact, it is very rare indeed that such unusual traits persist. That sterilization should follow as a punishment for sex crimes is without any sort of logic except that sterilization relates to sex. The whole idea is born of the hatred or loathing of certain crimes.

Generalizations have been made from a few poorly authenticated cases, and these generalizations have gone far beyond anything that the evidence can justify. It does not follow that because the father and son have black hair, or the mother and daughter have blue eyes, or that their mannerisms are similar, that inheritance is responsible for character, much less for crime. Certain things are clearly traceable to heredity. Other things may be the result of association or what to us must still be accident.

Often the fact is pointed out that great progress has been made in the culture of plants and the breeding of animals. This is true. No intelligent farmer to-day would think of raising any but the best stock. He takes pains with the breeding of his cattle. If he wants rich milk and butter, he breeds Jerseys or Guernseys. If he wants a larger quantity of milk and a fair beef animal, he breeds Holsteins. If he wants beef only, perhaps he raises Durhams. At any rate he knows what he wants and breeds that kind. Similarly the horse-raiser will breed for race horses or dray horses as the case may be, and the system works with almost mechanical certainty. He gets what he wants and would never think of raising scrubs and taking a chance on results. The effect of selective breeding and culture is beyond dispute, and to many it seems obvious that all that is needed to perfect the human race and wipe out misery and crime is to supervise human breeding in the same way, so that the species may be controlled.

At first glance this seems to be the logical thing to do, especially as the effects of heredity can no more be doubted in man than in animals. Still there are important questions to be asked and grave dangers to be encountered. When we say that the well-bred Berkshire hog is better than the "razor-back," we mean that it will produce more meat for food. In other words the hog is better for man. If we were to ask which would be the better, if the hog were to be considered, the answer would probably be the "razor-back." The fact that the food consumed by the Berkshire produces a large quantity of fat, makes him unfitted to live if he were living for his own sake. Turn both hogs out to run wild, and the "razor-back" will live and the Berkshire die. Nature will make her selection and adapt the hog to his environment. The Berkshire will produce more lard, but it will not run so fast; it has no more brains and cannot adapt what it has so well to the preservation of life. The same thing is doubtless true of other animals and likewise of plant life. The Jersey cow would not survive in a natural state. She gives too much milk and for too long a time. Man has made of her a milk-machine. Turn all thoroughbred horses out on the plains to shift for themselves, and they would either die or gradually be modified until they were adapted to the free and wild life of the plains. This would not be so good for man, but would be better for the horses.

In plants and animals, man can by selection breed or cultivate any characteristics that he may choose, but he cannot produce a horse which is both a draft horse and a running horse; he cannot produce cattle that are the best both for milk and beef. He is urged to try scientific breeding on the human race. How would he have man changed? Would he experiment for more intellect, or a bigger and stronger physique? Would he breed for art and civilization or would he breed for strength and physical endurance? What qualities are desirable for the human race? This would be a very hard question even to entrust to a popular vote. While the capacity of cattle to produce milk can be increased, cattle cannot increase their own capacity or improve their own quality. This can be done only by the slow and patient processes of Nature in the line of adapting the animal to its environment. The rapid change that is to come about by breeding must be directed and controlled by man. The cattle have nothing to say about the process. No doubt a higher order of beings who could control man might, and perhaps would change him by selective mating. How they would change him would depend on the use they wished to make of him, not on what the man himself would like to do. The contemplation of a higher order of beings experimenting with the human race is not a pleasant one for intelligent men.

Can we imagine men, through government, forcibly experimenting with each other? Who would settle the kind of man that was to be evolved or the specific changes that would be required? Or, what was to be done and how? Who could prophesy what man would be like when he should be made over in the likeness of something else? Who are the people with the breadth and tolerance and infinite wisdom, in whose hands it would be safe to place the remodeling of man? It is hard to conceive that it can be seriously considered.

Nature in her own way is a eugenist. By her slow processes she is continually wiping out the unfit and adapting man to the environment where he must live. Perhaps by saving too many of the unfit man is more or less interfering with the processes of Nature, and it may be that the interference with her method of work is bad. But Nature is mindful of this tendency and if it is not in accordance with the profoundest laws of being, Nature will have her way in spite of man's meddling. Any change that can be brought about by selective mating must come by natural processes aided by the education of each individual through a closer study of the origin and evolution of life. This must leave everyone free to do his own selecting, rather than to trust it to the state. Society can do much toward giving man an environment which will more or less be adjusted to his heredity. To give him a heredity that will conform to his environment is quite another thing and probably must be kept practically free from the theories, vagaries and experiments of man. It would seem so absurd and dangerous as not to be worth discussing except for the fact that the movement, both for sterilizing and some degree of control of mating has already gone far in some of the states. There is no limit that fanaticism or hatred will respect.

No doubt the popular opinion that in some way crime and pauperism are inherited has been strengthened by the literature concerning the family that has been given the name of "The Jukes." The first extensive study of this family was made by Richard L. Dugdale, who was connected with the New York Prison Association. It was first published in 1877 and may almost be regarded as the "Uncle Tom's Cabin" of the scientific study of crime in America.

Mr. Dugdale was evidently a careful student, an honest investigator and a humane man. Strange to say, deductions have been freely and carelessly made from his book, which the investigations do not warrant, and against which he carefully cautioned the reader. No one can examine Mr. Dugdale's book without being impressed with the quiet unassuming modesty and worth of the author, and yet in the hands of those who have so often carelessly and unscientifically generalized from his studies, it has possibly brought more harm than good.

The book covers investigations made by Dugdale between 1850 and 1870, a period in which little was known about the laws that govern inheritance, and necessarily, much evidence was pure hearsay without the data of careful investigation at hand. The case, however, does show a surprising number of criminals, paupers, harlots and misfits, descending from their original ancestor. From time to time further investigation has brought the history of the family down to 1918.

The ancestor with whom the investigation begins was born some time between 1720 and 1740. In the report the original is called "Max." He has been described as a "hunter and fisher," "a hard drinker," "not fond of work," fairly intelligent and leaving no record of crime. He probably left behind a large family, some of whom were legitimate and some illegitimate. The family came from a barren, rocky, lake region in New York and several generations grew up in the vicinity. The only industry was rough work like quarrying stone, logging and the like. Later a manufacturing plant was located in the region. The Jukes early got a bad name in the small community. Even when they wanted to find employment it was hard to get a job. They were socially ostracized and individually boycotted. The region was poor, and for the most part the family grew up in poverty. Often several members of a family lived in one room and slept on the floor indiscriminately, regardless of sex. For several generations few of them wandered far from the ancestral home. The locality was one that naturally came to be the resort of the poor and the outcast; these are always driven to the cheapest and most barren land. Whether the community was related by blood or not, the residents would almost inevitably be of the same class. Rich people cluster closely together for association and fellowship. The poor and wretched do the same. Common observation in city and country shows that this is inevitable. It comes from deeper and more fundamental laws than human statutes. It is born of the gregarious instinct and fostered and developed by economic law.

In the main, lax habits grow from surroundings and association. The tendency of all human beings is to revert to the primal. It is only association that keeps the individual units up to the tension that civilization expects and demands. Every community shows many examples of this inevitable tendency. Nature is constant; civilization spasmodic. Especially with sex relations, conditions are the chief factor. Nature knows little or nothing of the regulations fixed by society and custom. Poverty and wretchedness reach outward through a community and by association between the old and the young pass down the generations. Nothing but a complete change of environment can counteract the inevitable tendency. When social classes arise and the cleavage is clear and established, no great effort is made by the superior members to aid the inferior. In fact they are almost invariably left to themselves. Poverty and wretchedness are not transmitted in the blood, but in the environment.

It is not many years since physicians and communities believed that tuberculosis was inherited. In all communities there were instances of this dread disease spreading out through families and down the generations. It required the sacrifice of many lives and the careful investigation of scientists to discover that tuberculosis was the result of germs, generally accompanied by an impoverished system. These germs were transferred by close association and lack of sanitary conditions. It is as easy to transmit shiftlessness, idleness and lax habits as disease.

Dugdale's figures of delinquency in the Jukes family are doubtless much too high. A large percentage of facts was gained from gossip and hearsay about those long since dead. The details show that many crimes charged were not even proved, others were evidently not crimes, and in any small community suspicion would rest upon a member of this family who was accused. Then too, the poor in court and out have a hard time defending themselves. They are frequently convicted when accused. The evidence in regard to the subnormal and defective is still less satisfactory. Without close examination and thorough tests, illiteracy generally passes as subnormality. Very few of the subjects were submitted to a careful test. It is at least probable that this family was not much different from the other families who lived in like circumstances in the community.

Dugdale's original examination covered 709 cases out of about 1200 that were supposed to be living at the time. Of this number, 180 are put down as having received institutional and outdoor relief. The criminals and offenders are put down at 140. Habitual thieves convicted and unconvicted are listed at 60. Common prostitutes are put down at 50.

After Dugdale's investigation the family, from industrial and other conditions, became scattered and spread out over many states. A record has lately been made of the descendants of this family, the later record showing much improvement in the stock. This must be due to environment. It seems fairly certain that with time and opportunity, it will not much longer be a marked family.

Quite aside from the history, it seems certain that no results such as shown by Dugdale could have followed from inheritance. Defectiveness is a recessive factor; normality a dominant one. If such were not true, this would be a world of feeble-minded. If the Mendelian law held good in this regard, from a union of a defective and a normal person, three out of four would be normal, but as a matter of fact, the percentage of normal is no doubt much greater. It is only when both father and mother are feeble-minded that feeble-mindedness is sure to show in the offspring. With the modern care of this sort of defectives, the chance of breeding is growing rapidly less.

The Kallikak family is cited as another illustration showing the possible inheritance of criminality and poverty through a defective strain. This family, so far as shown, makes it still clearer that what some authors have charged to heredity is simply due to environment. These investigations do not show the need of controlling birth but do prove the necessity of improving environment. It is not possible to speak with certainty as to heredity and environment. The thorough investigation of these two factors which make up life is still in its infancy, but scientists are working out the problem, and we may be confident that with the right attitude toward crime, a remedy will be found for such cases as result from environment.

XXXIII

CRIME, DISEASE AND ACCIDENT

The criminologist has always looked for the cause of crime in some other direction than in the inherent wickedness of the criminal. Only those who make and enforce the law believe that men commit crimes because they choose the wrong.

Different writers have made their catalogues of causes that are responsible for crime, and most of these lists are more or less correct. There can be no doubt that more crimes against property are committed in cold weather than in warm weather; more in hard times than in good times; more by the unemployed than the employed; more during strikes and lockouts than in times of industrial peace; more when food is expensive and scarce than when it is cheap and plenty; more, in short, when it is harder to live. There is no doubt that there are more crimes of violence in extreme hot weather than in cold weather. That is, heat affects crimes as it affects disease and insanity and death; in short, as it affects all life. More crimes of violence are committed after wars or during heated political campaigns than at other times; more of such crimes when, either by climatic or other conditions, feelings are intensified or aroused and less subject to control. Likewise there are more crimes committed by young men between seventeen and twenty-four or five years of age than at any other age. Neither the very young nor the old commit crimes, except in rare cases. All the old people could be safely dismissed from prisons. Some few of the senile would need attention, and many need support and care, but none is dangerous to the community. There can be no question that practically all criminals are poor. Even when bankers get into prison they almost never have much money when they start that way, and none when they arrive. They are sent for something that would not have happened except for financial disaster. There is no longer any question that a large number, say probably from ten to twenty per cent of the convicted are, in fact, insane at the time the act was committed, and that the demented, the imbecile, and the clearly subnormal constitute many more than half of the inmates of prisons. Most of the rest can be accounted for by defective nervous systems, excessively strong instincts in some directions, weak ones in another, or a very hard environment. Add to this the facts that only a few have ever had any education worthy of the name, that most of them have never been trained to make a fair living by any trade or occupation, that almost all have had a poor early environment with no chance from the first, and most of them have had a very imperfect heredity. In short, sufficient statistics have been gathered and enough is known to warrant the belief that every case of crime could be accounted for on purely scientific grounds if all the facts bearing on the case were known.

Is there anything unreasonable in all of this? Is it outside of the other manifestations of life? Let us take disease. Clearly this is affected by heat and cold; beyond question it is largely the result of inherited susceptibilities. Poverty or wealth has much to do with disease. Many poor people die of tuberculosis, for instance, where the well-to-do would live. The span of life of the rich is greater than that of the poor. The long list of diseases from under-nourishment is mainly from the poor. Age affects disease, increasing the hazard of death. The food supply seriously affects health. Ignorance is a prolific cause of disease. Or, to speak more correctly, the lack of education and knowledge prevents men from living so that sickness will not overtake them, or so that they can recover when they are attacked by disease. The strength or weakness of the nervous system is a material factor.

The times of life, too, when the ravages of disease are greatest are as distinct as those of crime. And barring the fact that the few who are left at seventy rapidly drop away, the time of the greatest disasters would rather closely correspond with that of crime. Tuberculosis and insanity, for instance, take their greatest toll in the period of adolescence between fifteen and twenty-five years, just as crime does, and the percentage of both begins falling off rapidly after thirty.

Accidents can be as surely classified, and many of them in the same way. The poor naturally have more accidents than the rich; the ignorant more than the educated; the poorly-fed more than the well-nourished. Accidents are directly affected by climatic conditions; they are affected by human temperaments, by the strength and weakness of the nervous system, by the environment, by heredity, and by all the manifold stimuli that act on the human machine.

Legislatures have long since recognized that crime does not really stand as a separate and isolated phenomenon in human life. They have long since passed laws to safeguard the community against loss by accident and disease. A lengthening list of statutes can be found in our code regulating dangerous machinery, the operation of railroads, the running of automobiles, the construction of buildings, the isolation of the tubercular and those suffering from other contagious diseases, the amount of air-space for each person in tenement and work-shop, the use of fire-escapes and all of man's conduct and activity for the prevention of accidents and disease.

Quite apart from the question of the wisdom or the foolishness of all this line of legislative activity, over which there will always be serious discussion, it is evident that criminal conduct even now occupies no unique or isolated place in law or human conduct. All unconsciously the world is coming to look on all sorts of conduct either as social or anti-social, and this regardless of what has already been classified as criminal. A few years since science was absorbed in the study of man's racial origin and development. Today, biology and allied sciences are devoted to unraveling the complex causes responsible for individual development. It is fair to presume that this new effort of science may be able in time to solve the problem of crime, and that it may do for the conduct and mental aberrations of man what it has already done for his physical diseases.

XXXIV

LUCK AND CHANCE

Accident and luck may seem to have no place in a world of law, and yet the fate of lives rests almost entirely on what can be better classified under this head than any other.

This is a pluralistic universe. The world is made up of an infinite number of independent machines, each having its own existence and controlled by the laws of its own being. In going its several ways and living its own life, inevitably it often clashes with others and is seriously affected by them. The fox and the rabbit both roam the woods, apparently at will, at least independently of each other. By an infinite number of circumstances, at a particular time and place, their paths cross and the fox devours the rabbit. Had they not met at the time and place, the fate of the rabbit would not have been the same. The fox would have traveled farther and eaten another rabbit or some other animal in its stead.

An engine is running on a railroad track. It makes the trip day after day without accident or disaster. An automobile is one of a million built in a far-off city. Its mechanism is marvelous, and each part is dependent on the rest for its normal functioning. Some vital piece of the machine contains a flaw. How it chanced to be imperfect is another story involving endless speculation. An inherent natural defect in the ore, or a tired workman anywhere from the original smelting place to the last hand that touched it, may have been the cause; or, the reason may be still more impossible to discover. The machine is purchased and does its work perfectly for months. It is driven thousands of miles without any mishap. It is propelled along the highway and reaches the railroad track over which the engine runs. It is filled with happy people enjoying a vacation. The automobile and the engine reach the crossing at almost the same time. The automobile driver sees the engine and applies the brakes. For the first time since it left the shop, the machinery does not work. The car forges ahead and reaches the tracks just in time to be struck by the engine. The merry party meets disaster. No power could foresee the catastrophe, nor provide against the death that must result. Inevitably comes the clash of independent machines.

Each human being is a separate machine. Along the road of life he meets countless others like himself. Some chance meetings are fortunate and help the journey. Some other chance meeting with a human machine, a mechanical device, an infinitesimal microbe that happened to be at the same place at the same time brings disaster or death. This is luck or chance or fate, and this really hovers over every life, controlling its course and destiny and deciding when the puppet shall be laid away!

Luck and chance are the chief of all factors that really affect man. From birth to death the human machine is called on to make endless adjustments. A child is born and starts down the road of life. He starts blindly and, for the most part, travels the whole way in the mists and clouds. On his pathway he meets an infinite number of other pilgrims going blindly like himself. From the beginning to the end, all about him and in front of him are snares and pitfalls. His brain and nervous system are filled with emotions and desires which lure him here and there. Temptations are beckoning and passions urging him. He has no guide to show the way and no compass to direct his course. He knows that the journey will bring him to disaster in the end. He does not know the time or the nature of the last catastrophe he shall meet. Every step is taken in doubt and pain and fear. His friends and companions, through accident or disease, drop around him day by day. He cannot go back or halt or wait. He must go forward to the bitter end.

The whole journey of life is largely a question

of luck. Let anyone ask himself the question how often he has escaped disaster or how often death has just passed him by. How often has he done some act that would have led to degradation had it been known? How many hair-breadth escapes has he met? How many accidents has he had which luckily were slight but which easily might have caused his destruction?

Chance is the great element in life. Two men invest money; one gains a fortune, the other loses all. Two men are riding in a machine and it goes over a cliff; one is killed, the other escapes. The deadly germ is taken by one, it passes the other by; or, it is taken by one when his health will make him immune, by another at the time that it will destroy his life. How many temptations to violate the law has one just missed by a lucky accident? How many times has a previous experience, education, or a friend at the right time saved him from destruction?

The imperfect man travels this road; he is poor and friendless; his life is a long series of accidents great and small. The first accident that weakens his structure makes the second more certain and so on in increasing ratio until the end. Good luck crowds around one life, while ill luck and disaster follow another's footsteps wherever he goes with the persistency of his shadow.

In all the infinite number of chances one false

step may be enough to bring final disaster. All depends on the nature of the step. Every pilgrim makes innumerable false steps; often luck alone saves the situation; often luck alone compasses the destruction.

Insurance companies know just when accidents will befall the insured. If a man lives long enough he will die from a mischance. In a thousand men, a certain number will meet accident in a given time. It is just the same whether the insurance is written to be payable when a leg is cut off by a train or when money is embezzled from an employer. In either event the time can be figured out, and inevitably it will come if the time is long enough.

Neither is it necessary that the bad luck shall be great at the first misfortune. It may be but the loss of a few dollars which another could easily stand. It may be only a few days of sickness which would be of no consequence to someone else. It may be the death of a father or an uncle, while the same sort of tragedy might be the source of another's wealth. It may be some other person's hard luck which takes him from school and leaves him to follow a life of hard and constant toil. It may be that he had the bad luck not to marry the person of his choice, or it may be that he had the bad luck to marry her. It may be because he had no children; it may be because he had too many.

It may well be that he has been saved from prison by dying early of tuberculosis. He may have been saved from a railroad wreck by going to jail. Infinite are the tricks of chance. Infinite are the combinations and consequences that may come from turning the cards in a single deck.

Who is the perfect one that should be willing to punish vengefully his fellow-man? Let one look honestly into his own life and pick out the important things that lead to fortune or disaster from birth onward, and say how many are the results of circumstances over which he had no control.

Where is the human being, in the presence of a dead child or a dead parent or a dead friend or in the presence of a terrible trouble, that has not sat down in sorrow and despair and again and again lived over every circumstance that led to the disaster, asking why he did not turn this way instead of that way? Why did he not stop here, or go there; why did he do this or why did he not do that? Why did he not take this short step? Why did he not think of this or think of that? If only any one of almost an infinite number of things had been done or left undone, the dead would be alive or the disaster would not have befallen. Every man who is honest with himself knows that he has been a creature of conditions and chance, or at least what is chance as far as a man can see, and what was clearly chance to him. He knows that if he has met success, he has only been more in luck than the rest. If he has intelligence and human sympathy, he feels only pity for the suffering. He would never punish in vengeance or hatred. He knows that all do the best they can, with what they have.

Enumerating some of the many causes of crime ought to be an unnecessary task. To give the number of ways men die or are killed by accident, means only that sooner or later they die, and if they had not died one way, they would have died another. It means only that a machine will inevitably give way in some part, and man may go on finding the weak spots and strengthening them forever and still the end will come. Fate does not look for a weak spot; it looks for the weakest and finds it.

Manifold causes produce crime; some men commit it from one cause: some from another. Statistics only show the number of men who commit crime from the various separate causes. In logic and philosophy it really shows that, a certain heredity placed in a certain environment, will meet obstructions and obstacles. Some heredities will carry men further, and some environments will overcome them more quickly; but as surely as effects follow from causes, every heredity will meet disaster in some way under any environment, and the time and kind of disaster it meets depend not upon perverseness or freedom of will, but upon the fortune of the meeting of heredity with the manifold environment that surrounds every life. It must be plain that life lasts only as long as it makes adjustments. That it consists only of adjustments. That, ordinarily, strong heredity and a good environment will serve the longest. That, generally, a weak heredity and a poor environment will meet disaster soonest. Life may be lengthened either by improving the heredity or the environment or both. Whatever catastrophe overtakes it and the time it falls depend not upon the will of the machine, but upon the character of the machine that starts on the journey and the road it travels. The disasters cannot in reason or justice be divided into criminal or non-criminal. They are all natural; they are each and all inevitable. Each is the inevitable destruction of a machine which could stand so much, but which could stand no more. And in each, in spite of both heredity and the general environment, the constant meeting with other machines due to pure luck and chance is a great factor, if not the chief factor, that determines the individual life.

XXXV

PARDONS AND PAROLES

It has always been the province of the Chief Executive of a state or nation to grant pardons or clemency to those who are confined in prison. This is largely to correct the mistakes of courts and juries and is often indulged in by presidents and governors at Christmas time. Experience shows that during the trial of a case, especially one that causes public notice and general discussion, injustice is frequently done. Often the defendant is convicted when he should have been acquitted, and still more frequently punishments are excessive and cruel. Almost never is any serious inquiry made as to the heredity and environment of the accused. Probably trial by jury has served to save many defendants where the judge would have convicted, and has still more often tempered and modified penalties. Still, juries are by no means free from the mob psychology that surrounds and affects most important and well-known cases. Jurors are generally none too intelligent and not very ready to stand against public opinion. Most men agree with the crowd. The prevailing religious opinion and the dominant political and social ideas are accepted and believed by the ordinary citizen. Social and business considerations cause most men to go with the crowd, and in any case of importance it is easy for a jury to tell the feeling of the populace. If the case has attracted much attention, the juror knows the prevailing ideas as to the guilt or innocence of the defendant. When he takes his seat in the box he almost always shares that feeling. If the case is not one he has heard of or discussed, he can easily tell by the actions and surroundings of the court room how public feeling lies. All lawyers know how readily men feel the sentiment of a court room and how much easier is the task when the sentiment is their way. Juries are also apt to have an undue regard for the opinion of the judge. In spite of the fact that it is their province to pass upon the facts, they are very watchful of all the judge says and does and are prone to decide a case as they believe the judge wishes it to be decided. Even when the judge is not permitted to express any opinions on the facts involved, it is difficult for him to hide his real feelings, and when his desire is strong for either side it is easy to make his opinions known.

A jury is more apt to be unbiased and independent than a court, but they very seldom stand up against strong public clamor. Judges naturally believe the defendant is guilty. They feel that the fact that an indictment has been found is a strong presumption against the accused. The judge regards himself as a part of the administration of justice and feels that it is a part of his duty to see that no guilty man escapes. Generally, in the administration of the court he is very closely connected with the state's attorney and naturally believes that the attorney would not have procured an indictment, much less pushed a trial, unless the defendant was guilty.

The whole atmosphere of the court at the time of the trial calls for a harsher and more drastic dealing with a defendant than would naturally prevail after the feeling has passed away. For this reason, the pardoning power is given to the chief executive to correct errors or undue harshness after the legal proceedings have been finished. Often after months or years, the persons or family who have suffered at the hands of the defendant feel like reversing their judgment or extending charity, and it is not unusual that the prosecutor and judge who conducted the case ask for leniency and a mitigation of the sentence is imposed. So often is an appeal made and so frequently is it felt just to grant clemency, that this part of the duty of the chief executive has grown to be very burdensome and really impossible for him thoroughly to perform. The policy of the law is further to give a prisoner some consideration and in cases of good behavior and mitigating circumstances to release him before the expiration of his time. In most states this has called for the creating of a board of pardons and parole. The statutes fixing penalties for certain offenses provide for a reduction of a certain number of weeks or months each year, but as a rule courts take this provision into consideration and figure out the net time they wish to give the defendant so that there is no clemency except through pardon or parole.

In most states the duties of the board are very grave and its business large. With this has generally gone a law providing for the release of prisoners on parole before their sentences are finished. In these cases the prisoner is paroled to someone who promises the board to employ him, and a monthly report is to be made of his conduct for a stated length of time. He is then given conditional freedom, subject to the revocation of the parole by the board on the violation of its terms.

The administration of this power has made the parole board one of the most important, if not the most important, of any branch of the state government. The lives and well-being of thousands of prisoners are absolutely dependent on this board. Even more important are the happiness and well-being of the families of the inmates of the prison. The power and responsibilities of this board are so great that only men of the best judgment and of humane and just tendencies should be trusted with the task. It also calls for great courage such as few men on boards possess. The public generally clamors for vengeance and unfairly and unjustly criticises the board, especially when a released man violates his parole or commits another crime. This frequently happens. Perhaps on an average ten per cent of those paroled are sent back to prison before their term expires. All this makes it hard for the board to perform its duties, and makes the members of the board timid and doubtful of the result, often causing them to deny paroles in many cases where they should be given.

A great deal of criticism has been made of the parole system. Public officials and that part of the crowd that is clamorous for vengeance are always ready to assail its activities unfairly and unduly. Most professional criminals are against the parole board. Speaking of the State of Illinois, I am sure that the parole law, instead of shortening the time of imprisonment, has lengthened the terms. All lawyers in any way competent to handle the defense of a criminal case would, in the event of conviction, almost always get a shorter term for their clients from a jury or from the court, or even from the prosecutor, than from the parole board. I feel strongly that the board is too timid and unwilling to grant paroles. Still in spite of this there can be no doubt that the parole law is a step in the right direction, and it should be upheld by all who believe offenders should have a better chance. If human nature in the administration of law could be relied on; if there were some method of getting men of courage and capacity with plenty of competent aid and assistance to take charge of paroles and prisons, then the ideal sentence should be one that fixed no time whatever. It should simply leave a prisoner for study and observation until it was thought wise and safe to release him from restraint. This like all the rest could not be done with the present public attitude toward criminals. So long as men subscribe to the prevailing idea of crime and punishment, no officials could stand up against public opinion in the carrying out of a new and radical theory, and even if such a board should be established, the law under which it acted would soon be repealed or the members of the board forced to resign and a new one would take its place.

In spite of the fact that the effect of parole boards has been to lengthen sentences, and in spite of my personal belief that they should be materially shortened, I am confident that the parole system should be maintained with the hope of improvement and the chance of gradually educating the public until sentences can be naturally shortened, and the care and control of prisoners be placed on a scientific and humane basis.

A board of pardons and paroles should be made

up of men who are really interested in their work. They should carefully keep up with the literature on crime and punishment; they should be scientists in all matters touching their work, and they should be men of humane feelings. It is too much to expect that all of this can be found in a board for a long time to come, but with good sense and the right attitude of mind the board could employ the skill that it does not now have. Every prisoner should be the subject of attention, not of spying, but of friendly interest that would inspire confidence and trust,—such an interest as a wise doctor has in a patient. This attention would in most cases gain the confidence of the prisoner and make it possible to find out how far he could be trusted, at the same time showing the treatment and environment he needed for future development. Where this confidence could not be had, safety would probably require a longer term. Most men respond to kind treatment. The criminal has so long looked on the world as his enemy, especially the official world, that he hesitates to trust anyone. Still the really sympathetic and kindly man who is honestly trying to help him will sooner or later get his confidence and coöperation. Every prisoner should understand that all of those around him are anxious to educate him so as to fit him for society and to put him in an environment where he can live. Even then there would be mistakes, and a portion of the prisoners would be so defective or imperfect that they never could be released; but under proper treatment many would be restored to association with their fellow-men.

It will be a long time before it will be safe to make sentences entirely indeterminate. Boards cannot be trusted to give such time and work and judgment to their task as will prevent cases of great injustice. Until such time shall come either the statutes must fix an unbending and arbitrary time which takes no account of individual cases, or it must be left with the court or jury. Clearly the jury should fix the maximum, leaving the members of the board to reduce the penalty if they deem it wise.

Most men are forgotten when they go to prison, especially if they have no active friends on the outside. No board can fully keep in mind all the inmates of a large prison. It may be that by some system their attention is automatically called to the man at certain times, but this matters very little. Someone should know he is there and why, and who he is. He should not be an abstract, but a concrete man. For these reasons, a limit should always be set on a punishment and the limit should not be too long. The idea of a tribunal, perhaps including the judge who passed sentence, having the power and the duty imposed upon him to review sentences and reduce them if it seemed best from time to time, might have a good effect. The feelings of most men in reference to the degree of punishment change as time goes by. Always with the punishment is a strong feeling of both hate and fear. It is not possible really to punish, that is, to inflict suffering without hate or fear. The most necessary thing in preparing soldiers to fight, is to teach them to hate and fear the enemy. In the trial of a case, these feelings are fresh in the minds of the prosecutor and the judge when the case is finished, and they necessarily act more or less under the dominance of their passions. In time these feelings fade, and a saner and kindlier judgment takes the place of the first feelings that possessed the mind.

With the parole system is going on a movement for probation. This provides that the convicted man need not be sent to prison but may be released on certain terms, sometimes requiring that money taken shall be refunded. After that he shall be placed under the supervision of some friend or agent who will report from time to time to probation officers or to the court. Probation is generally granted to young prisoners and first offenders but usually not permitted in cases that the law classifies as the most serious.

Parole and probation are much the same in theory. In both these cases the clemency should depend much more upon the man than on the crime. It does not follow that a very serious crime shows a poorer moral fibre than a lesser one. It may well be that the seemingly slight transgressions, like stealing small amounts, picking pockets and the like, show a really weaker nature than goes with a more heroic crime. There is no such liability to repeat in homicide as there is in forgery, pocket-picking or swindling. The seriousness of a homicide is likely to make it impossible that the same man shall ever kill again. Many such men would be perfectly safe on probation or parole. But the smaller things that are easily concealed and come from an effort of the condemned to live, either without work or in a better way than his ability or training permits him to do in the hard and unfair conditions that society imposes, are often much harder to overcome. At any rate, the main question should be in regard to the man and not the crime. In cases of parole or probation, society should do what it can to help the man make good. Generally employment is necessary and a different and easier environment often indispensable. If organized society would only take the pains to make an easier environment for all the less favored, the problem would be fairly simple and most of the misery that comes from crime and prison would gradually disappear.

XXXVI

REMEDIES

Students of crime and punishment have never differed seriously in their conclusions. All investigations have arrived at the result that crime is due to causes; that man is either not morally responsible, or responsible only to a slight degree. All have doubted the efficacy of punishment and practically no one has accepted the common ideas that prevail as to crime, its nature, its treatment and the proper and efficient way of protecting society from the criminal.

The real question of importance is: What shall be done? Can crime be cured? If not, can it be wiped out and how? What rights have the public? What rights has the criminal? What obligations does the public owe the criminal? What duties does each citizen owe society?

It must be confessed that all these questions are more easily asked than answered. Perhaps none of them can be satisfactorily answered. It is a common obsession that every evil must have a remedy; that if it cannot be cured today, it can be tomorrow; that man is a creature of infinite possibilities and all that is needed is time and patience. Given these a perfect world will eventuate.

I am convinced that man is not a creature of infinite possibilities. I am by no means sure that he has not run his race and reached, if not passed, the zenith of his power. I have no idea that every evil can be cured; that all trouble can be banished; that every maladjustment can be corrected or that the millennium can be reached now and here or any time or anywhere. I am not even convinced that the race can substantially improve. Perhaps here and there society can be made to run a little more smoothly; perhaps some of the chief frictions incident to life may be avoided; perhaps we can develop a little higher social order; perhaps we may get rid of some of the cruelty incident to social organization. But how?

To start with: it seems to me to be clear that there is really no such thing as crime, as the word is generally understood. Every activity of man should come under the head of "behavior." In studying crime we are merely investigating a certain kind of human behavior. Man acts in response to outside stimuli. How he acts depends on the nature, strength, and inherent character of the machine and the habits, customs, inhibitions and experiences that environment gives him. Man is in no sense the maker of himself and has no more power than any other machine to escape the law of cause and effect. He does as he must. Therefore, there is no such thing as moral responsibility in the sense in which this expression is ordinarily used. Punishment as something inflicted for the purpose of giving pain is cruelty and vengeance and nothing else. Whatever should be done to the criminal, if we have humanity and imagination, we must feel sympathy for him and consider his best good along with that of all the rest of the members of the society whose welfare is our concern.

While punishment cannot be defended, still self-defense is inherent in both individuals and society and, without arguing its justification, no one can imagine a society that will not assert it and act for its defense. This will be true regardless of whether the given society is worth preserving or not. Inherent in all life and organization is the impulse of self-preservation. Those members of society who are sufficiently "anti-social" from the standpoint of the time and place will not be tolerated unduly to disturb the rest. These, in certain instances, will be destroyed or deprived of their power to harm. If society has a right attitude toward the subject, if it has imagination and sympathy and understanding, it will isolate these victims, not in anger but in pity, solely for the protection of the whole. Some there are who ask what difference it makes whether it is called punishment or not. I think that the attitude of society toward the criminal makes the whole difference, and any improvement is out of the question until this attitude influences and controls the whole treatment of the question of crime and punishment.

If doctors and scientists had been no wiser than lawyers, judges, legislatures and the public, the world would still be punishing imbeciles, the insane, the inferior and the sick; and treating human ailments with incantations, witchcraft, force and magic. We should still be driving devils out of the sick and into the swine.

Assuming then that man is governed by external conditions; that he inevitably reacts to certain stimuli; that he is affected by all the things that surround him; that his every act and manifestation is a result of law; what then must we and can we do with and for the criminal?

First of all we must abandon the idea of working his moral reformation, as the term "moral reformation" is popularly understood. As well might we cure the physically ill in that way! Man works according to his structure. He never does reform and cannot reform. As he grows older his structure changes and from increase of vitality or from decrease of vitality his habits, too, may change. He may likewise learn by experience, and through the comparing and recalling of experiences and their consequences may build up rules of conduct which will restrain him from doing certain things that he otherwise would do. Anything that increases his knowledge and adds to his experience will naturally affect his habits and will either build up or tear down inhibitions or do both, as the case may be. If he has intelligence he knows he is always the same man; that he has not reformed nor repented. He may regret that he did certain things but he knows why and how he did them and why he will not repeat them if he can avoid it. The intrinsic character of the man cannot change, for the machine is the same and will always be the same, except that it may run faster or slower with the passing years, or it may be influenced by the habits gained from experience and life.

We must learn to appraise rightly the equipment of every child and, as far as possible, of every adult to the end that they may find an environment where they can live. It must never be forgotten that man is nothing but heredity and environment and that the heredity cannot be changed but the environment may be. In the past and present, the world has sought to adjust heredity to environment. The problem of the future in dealing with crime will be to adjust environment to heredity. To a large extent this can be done in a wholesale way. Any improved social arrangement that will make it easier for the common man to live will necessarily save a large number from crime. Perhaps if the social improvement should be great enough it would prevent the vast majority of criminal acts. Life should be made easier for the great mass from which the criminal is ever coming. As far as experience and logic can prove anything, it is certain that every improvement in environment will lessen crime.

Codes of law should be shortened and rendered simpler. It should not be expected that criminal codes will cover all human and social life. The old method of appealing to brute force and fear should gradually give place to teaching and persuading and fitting men for life. All prisons should be in the hands of experts, physicians, criminologists, biologists, and, above all, the humane. Every prisoner should be made to feel that the state is interested in his good as well as the good of the society from which he came. Sentences should be indeterminate, but the indeterminate sentence of today is often a menace to freedom and a means of great cruelty and wrong. The indeterminate sentence can only be of value in a well-equipped prison where each man is under competent observation as if he were ill in a hospital. And this should be supplemented with an honest, intelligent parole commission, fully equipped for thorough work. Until that time comes, the maximum penalty should be fixed by the jury, the parole board retaining the power to reduce the punishment or parole. No two crimes are alike. No two offenders are alike. Those who have no friends on the outside are forgotten and neglected after the prison doors have been closed upon them. Some men now are confined much too long; others not long enough. No doubt, owing to the imperfections of man, this will always be the case.

At present no penal institutions have the equipment or management to provide against such shortcomings. They never can have it while men believe punishment is vengeance. When the public is ready to provide for the protection of society and still to recognize and heed the impulses of humanity and mercy, it will abolish all fixed terms. As well might it send a patient to a hospital for a fixed time and then discharge him, regardless of whether he is cured or not, as to confine a convict for a definite predetermined time. If the offense is one of a serious nature that endangers the public, the prisoner should not be released until by understanding or education, or age, or the proper form of treatment, it is fairly evident that he will not offend again. When the time comes, if it is the day of his incarceration, he should be released. The smallest reflection ought to teach that for many crimes, especially for many property crimes, it is hopeless to release a prisoner in an environment where he cannot survive. An environment adjusted to his heredity must be found by the state.

All indignities should be taken away from prison life. Instead the prisoner should be taught that his act was the necessary result of cause and effect and that, given his heredity and environment, he could have done no other way. He should by teaching and experience be shown where he made his mistakes, and he should be given an environment where he can live consistently with the good of those around him.

Various reforms have been urged in the treatment of criminals and in criminal procedure in the courts. Most of these impress me as possessing no fundamental value. It is often said that the accused should be given an immediate trial; that this and subsequent proceedings should not be hindered by delay; that the uncertainties of punishment furnish the criminal with the hope of escape and therefore do not give the community the benefit of the terror that comes with the certainty of punishment that could prevent crime. I can see no basis in logic or experience for this suggestion. It is based on the theory that punishment is not only a deterrent to crime, but the main deterrent. It comes from the idea that the criminal is distinct from the rest of mankind, that vengeance should be sure and speedy and that then crime would be prevented. If this were true and the only consideration to prevent crime, then the old torture chamber and the ancient prison with all its hopelessness and horror should be restored. Logic, humanity and experience would protest against this. If there is to be any permanent improvement in man and any better social order, it must come mainly from the education and humanizing of man. I am quite certain that the more the question of crime and its treatment is studied the less faith men have in punishment.

England and Continental Europe are often pointed to as examples of sure and speedy justice. The fact that there are more convictions and fewer acquittals in England in proportion to the number of trials does not prove that the English system is better than ours. It may and probably does mean that ours is better. Here the accused has more chance. There the expense, the formality, the power of the court all conspire to destroy every opportunity of escape, regardless of innocence or guilt. Even the fact that there are fewer crimes committed in England does not prove that the system is best or that it prevents crime. An old country with its life of caste lacks the freedom and equality that naturally produce defiance of rules and customs and lead to breaches of the law. Other things being equal, a greater degree of freedom leads to more violations of rules and greater resisting power among the poor than a lesser degree of freedom. It does not necessarily follow that the country is best where the people are the most obedient. Complete obedience leads to submission, to aggression and to despotism. Doubtless China has fewer crimes than England. The power of resistance is so crushed that no one thinks of defying a master, resenting an injury, violating a rule, claiming any personal rights or protesting against caste, age, or privilege.

Always there are certain men who believe that all reform in criminal procedure must come by abolishing juries and submitting every question to a court. Those who are rich and strong and the lawyers who advocate their interests are mainly arrayed on this side. The poor and rebellious, with those who naturally or otherwise advocate their cause, stand for the juries as against the courts. Those who strive to be fair are often misled from a lack of experience and little judgment of human nature. The public is always against the accused. The press is against him. The machinery of the law is against him. The dice are loaded for his conviction. Some people have childish faith in the courts. But judges are neither infinitely wise nor infinitely good; they come from the ranks of lawyers and for the most part from those who have been long engaged in defending property rights; they are generally conservative; they are not independent of public opinion; almost invariably they reflect public opinion, which means the public opinion of the community in which they live. Few of them have much knowledge of biology, of psychology, of sociology, or even of history.

One curse of our political life comes from the fact that as soon as a man has secured an office, he has his eye on another and his whole effort is to please the people, that is, the people who express themselves the most easily. Very few judges rise to a great degree of independence or defy popular clamor. A jury is less bound by public opinion; their responsibility is divided; they are not as a rule seeking office; while swayed by the crowd they are still more independent than judges and with them the common man, the accused, has a better chance.

No doubt judges are abler, better educated, more accustomed to weighing evidence and able to arrive at a more logical conclusion than most juries. Still none of these qualities necessarily leads to just findings. Questions of right and wrong are not determined by strict rules of logic. If public opinion could come to regard the criminal as it does the insane, the imbecile, or the ill, then a judicial determination would be the best. But as long as crime is regarded as moral delinquency and punishment savors of vengeance, every possible safeguard and protection must be thrown around the accused. In the settling of opinions and the passing of judgments, mob psychology is all-powerful and really, in the last analysis, every human question comes down to the power of public opinion.

The first thing necessary to lessen crime and to relieve victims from the cruelty of moral judgments is a change of public opinion as to human responsibility. When scientific ideas on this important subject shall be generally accepted, all things that are possible will follow from it. Some headway has already been made in the direction of considering heredity and environment. Theoretically we no longer hold the insane responsible, and some allowance is made for children and the obviously defective. The discouraging thing is that the public is fickle and changeable, and any temporary feeling overwhelms the patient efforts of years. In the present mad crusade against crime consequent upon the Great War, penalties have been increased, new crimes created, and paroles and pardons have been made almost impossible. The public and press virtually declare that even insanity should not save the life of one who slays his fellow. Repeatedly the insane are hanged without a chance, and sentences of death are pronounced, where before, a term of years, or life imprisonment would have been the penalty for the offense. Individual men and collections of men are ruled not by judgment but by impulse; the voice of conscience and mercy is always very weak and drowned by the hoarse cry for vengeance.

As long as men collectively impose their will

upon the individual units, they should consider that this imposition calls for intelligence, kindliness, tolerance and a large degree of sympathy and understanding. In considering the welfare of the public: the accused, his family and his friends should be included as a part. It need not be expected that all maladjustments can ever be wiped out. Organization with its close relation of individual units implies conflict. Nevertheless, the effort should be to remove all possible inducement for the violent clashing of individuals and to minimize the severity of such conflicts as are inevitable.

THE END

INDEX

Published by

Facsimile Publisher
Ashok Vihar, Delhi-110052 (India)
Website: www.facsimilepublisher.com

Distributed by

GYAN

Gyan Books Pvt. Ltd.
5, Ansari Road, Daryaganj, New Delhi-110002 (India)
E-mail: books@gyanbooks.com, Website: www.gyanbooks.com

2 222000 007683